DUCT TAPE
SELLING

ALSO BY JOHN JANTSCH

Duct Tape Marketing: The World's Most Practical Small Business Marketing Guide

The Referral Engine: Teaching Your Business to Market Itself

The Commitment Engine: Making Work Worth It

DUCT TAPE

SELLING

THINK LIKE A MARKETER, SELL LIKE A SUPERSTAR

JOHN JANTSCH

PORTFOLIO / PENGUIN

PORTFOLIO / PENGUIN

Published by the Penguin Group
Penguin Group (USA) LLC
375 Hudson Street
New York, New York 10014

USA | Canada | UK | Ireland | Australia | New Zealand | India | South Africa | China
penguin.com
A Penguin Random House Company

First published by Portfolio / Penguin, a member of Penguin Group (USA) LLC, 2014

ISBN 978-1-59184-633-8

Printed in the United States of America
1 3 5 7 9 10 8 6 4 2

Set in Minion Pro
Designed by Elyse Strongin

To Robert W. Jantsch,
my father and first sales coach

CONTENTS

Introduction:
Changing the Context of Selling

Success Is Often Mostly About Context

On a cold January morning in 2007, a hidden video camera captured thousands of commuters simply walking past violinist Joshua Bell as he played some of the most complex music ever written, on an extremely valuable Stradivarius violin. Most didn't seem to notice the difference between Bell's virtuosity and the skill of an everyday subway musician.

Just days before, and then again after this experiment, Bell performed to sold-out theaters filled with ticket holders willing to pay top dollar and ready to deliver thunderous standing ovations.

In the context of the subway station, ordinary people did not recognize Bell's genius.

We don't live in a vacuum. Every idea we have, song we hear, or sales pitch we connect with is filtered through a number of elements, including our mood, the environment, and our unique understanding of the world and our place in it. All of these factors affect the value and importance we place on what we believe in, what we deem worthy of our time, and what we buy.

In the same vein, while salespeople's mastery, skill, or point of view may be important and well thought-out, the context in which their ideas, introductions, and pitches are delivered is equally—or sometimes more—important.

In many ways this book is about changing the context of how you, as a salesperson, are received and perceived.

So let me ask you this: Are you ready to hone your virtuosity as a salesperson and put it on display in the places where people willingly pay a premium to engage such work or are you content to hang around in the subway hoping for the scraps of interested passersby?

Change Your Context, Change Your Results

This book is designed to show you, first, how to reframe your own mindset about what it means to sell in the world today. From there, we'll look at how to vastly alter the way prospects, customers, and competitors view your professional brand. To do so, you need to think of yourself as a *guide* in the customer's buying process rather than an information source, research data point, transaction catalyst, or whatever other trendy term people have assigned to the act of selling.

This book will show you how to change the context of selling by teaching you how to:

- Ask what you can give your clients instead of asking what they can give you
- Form and lead an industry group instead of mindlessly joining every one you find
- Make education-rich sales pitches to rooms packed with engaged potential clients instead of cold-calling prospects
- Get yourself invited to speak in front of audiences instead of simply attending events
- Earn the trust to be introduced to referral prospects instead of given leads
- Interview industry luminaries instead of simply downloading their podcasts
- Build a strategic-partner network instead of waiting around to be asked to partner
- Write for respected industry publications instead of just putting them in your RSS reader

When you reframe any relationship, you often change the way you are heard, received, and perceived. In sales, by reframing the selling process as a journey that you and the client are on together—and that you are guiding him through—you can become a valuable and necessary part of your client's team.

About This Book

Duct Tape Selling is divided into three parts. The first two parts are "Mind-set of the New Sales Guide" and "Practices of the New Sales Guide." Part I is aimed squarely at equipping the individual salesperson with the mind-set that will enable you to act as a guide for your prospects and clients in the buying process. You can think of it as laying the foundation for your new sales strategy. The second part offers the very practical new skills and techniques you must master to take full advantage of the new selling environment. You'll find that the mind-sets and processes I write about are often traditionally thought of as belonging to marketers rather than sellers. The new sales world no longer supports those distinctions. To succeed, sellers must understand the marketing mind-set.

If you are an independent salesperson, you can adopt these new strategies and tactics as you work your way through this book. I encourage you to take action on some element of every chapter—you'll find a lot of ideas you can begin to implement immediately, ideas that set the groundwork for long-term success while also providing short-term results.

If you're charged with leading a sales department or organization, you'll find the third part, "The World of the New Sales Coach," particularly valuable. This section is intended for the business owner, VP of sales, or sales manager charged with hiring, training, equipping, and incentivizing the new sales guide model in a team setting. Here, I'll reveal how you, as a sales manager, can adapt a coaching mentality to train others in the new model of selling. The effectiveness, as well as the implementation, of the new selling mind-set and tools is governed to a large extent by the acceptance and practice of this third part by those in leadership positions.

If you work for a sales organization and the ideas in this book resonate with you, but conflict with the way your organization views the sales function, I urge you to share this book with your boss. You can be the key driver in reframing the context of the sales function internally and externally.

How This Book Came About

Before we go any further, I think it's important that I share my inspiration for writing this book.

I've been a marketing consultant and small-business owner for over twenty-five years, and in that time I've worked with just about every industry imaginable. I've worked with solo entrepreneurs charged with every aspect of marketing and sales, and with very large organizations struggling to get sales and marketing departments to think and speak in the same language.

Prior to starting my own marketing firm, I was employed as a sales rep for a national printing company and spent my days knocking on doors and building relationships. It was in that role that I discovered firsthand the power of stepping *outside* the normal bounds of sales tactics.

I found that if I communicated more directly with customers, sent letters, postcards, and handwritten notes (this was before e-mail, mind you), shared important new bits of information, spotted some new channel they could use to grow their business, or simply took note of something they did that struck me, I was a welcome sight at their door, instead of a nuisance.

Thanks to these practices, I not only outsold everyone else in my organization, I was asked to create a complete marketing program for the rest of the sales team and further tasked with teaching the sales management team to think like marketers. Even then I realized that the best salespeople thought like marketers—perhaps even more effectively than the folks responsible for marketing activities.

Now, keep in mind that this was almost thirty years ago. While the Internet has heightened the need for change, it didn't actually cause it! The line between sales and marketing was blurring before the Internet's rise, although the pace of that breakdown has obviously increased. So while the system that I outline in this book employs every up-to-date tactic available, it draws first from the mind-set of delivering value above all. The most successful sales professionals have long understood that, regardless of the sales environment, the sales professional who adds value wins.

My father, an independent manufacturers representative for most of his working life, was the first to demonstrate to me the direct correlation between delivering value and success as a sales professional. When I started developing my own marketing system and applied it to the act of selling, I saw how effective merging these two ideas could be.

Since then I've written three books on the topics of marketing, referral generation, and overall business strategy. Each book—*Duct Tape Marketing, The Referral Engine,* and *The Commitment Engine*—highlights some aspect of blending marketing and sales that delivers value to the end customer while remaining terribly practical for the business owner and sales team. With this book, however, I address that blending head-on.

Most people already know that the days of knocking on doors and hard selling are over. But as I travel around the world speaking to groups of business owners, marketers, and sales professionals, the number one question I'm asked is, "What do we do now? How can we sell successfully in this new world?"

I've written this book specifically to answer that question. At the heart of it, marketing and sales have become activities that no longer simply support each other so much as feed off of each other's activity. Sales professionals must think and act like marketers in order to completely reframe their role in the mind of the customer. And marketers also need to pay attention and adjust to their changing roles, working with the sales department or reps in a way they've never had to before.

The way forward for sales success is to think like a marketer, sell like a superstar. To do so, let's look at the first set—changing your mind-set.

Let's go to work!

PART I

MIND-SET OF THE NEW SALES GUIDE

Why Marketing Is the New Selling

In the traditional model, marketing owned the message of any given business, while sales owned the relationships.

The sales team often had little impact on the way marketing messages were developed and, correspondingly, marketing often had little interaction with the end customer. While this distinction might have served the organization in terms of roles and responsibilities, it rarely led to the type of collaborative approach demanded by today's customer.

In order to thrive in our digitally driven business environment, a salesperson needs to think and act more like a marketer. Although I suppose this has always been true to some degree, it is painfully true now that prospective clients have access to mounds of information, tools to deflect unwanted sales messages, and the ability to freely publish both flattering and unflattering information about the companies with which they choose to do business.

In order to succeed, salespeople need to take matters into their own hands and connect much more deeply with the marketing side of the business. Sales, as much as marketing, needs to have input into and control over the organization's message. I've often said that getting marketing and sales on the same page was one of the biggest challenges for departmentalized business, but now it's become a necessary challenge for the individual as well.

In the new business model, there can be little distinction between who owns the message and who owns the relationship. Marketing must improve its relationship building and sales must get better at message building and delivery.

Surely you've seen the art of selling evolve tremendously over the last few years. This is in large part because markets now have immediate and deep access to the kind of information once delivered as a primary function of the selling process.

For the individual salesperson this means the following elements of selling have changed:

Listening Is the New Prospecting

While it has become much more difficult to gain access to prospects via phone and e-mail, it's actually become much easier to *understand* the individual needs of a prospect, due in large part to social media.

Salespeople need to create their own socially driven listening stations, add social profiles to their customer relationship management (CRM) tools, and stay on top of what customers and competitors are doing.

When you listen actively instead of prospecting, you'll find that potential and existing customers will voluntarily—and publicly—scatter sales clues.

Educating Is the New Presenting

Formerly, salespeople were encouraged to perfect their pitch. Pitching was the primary sales mechanism, and many sales training courses still teach it. But in reality, over time the pitch became little more than an effective manipulation strategy, full of proven psychological principles and gimmicks.

Today's salesperson must be ready to teach, publish, and demonstrate his or her expertise. You should be ready to answer questions via blog posts, engage in social media conversations, and conduct online and offline seminars as a way of educating prospects.

It is very hard for salespeople to turn the pitch off once they are used to relying on it 24/7, but the ones who do are reaping the benefits.

Insight Is the New Information Sharing

Prospects have access to the best information in the world at the mere click of a button. They have access to everything we sales professionals share online, as well as what our competitors, customers, and partners share about us and the industry in general.

In collecting information, prospects can either become very smart or very confused about what's being sold. Today's salesperson must act as a filter for the mass of available information and provide insight, context, and guidance about it. Your role is to help prospects understand the questions they need to consider, and then provide the answers. To do so, you must be very good at helping prospects aggregate, filter, and condense the mass of information. In effect, you must become more like a guide in the process of selling.

Story Building Is the New Nurturing

Stories are the greatest relationship builders. As Mister Rogers used to say, "It's hard not to like someone once you know their story."

The job of storytelling is collaborative. Salespeople must first be able to relate the organization's core stories to the world of the customer, then help the customer build a new story, with salespeople taking the leading role and solving the customer's problems.

Conclusive story building is only accomplished with proof over promise. Today's salesperson must actively understand, measure, and communicate the real results that customers achieve in every engagement. And they must bring those real-life stories to new customers and prospects.

Value Delivery Is the New Closing

Whenever I hear the word "closing," all I can think of is Alec Baldwin's epic "always be closing" speech in the film *Glengarry Glen Ross*. But that view doesn't work today—the modern salesperson must instead "always be building value."

I'm not saying that closed deals don't count. They do, and your success as a salesperson depends on that metric. But sticking with the mind-set of adding value over the pressure to close at any cost is the difference between the old and the new.

If you can deliver value (and education) to your client, traditional closing tactics become a thing of the past. And this isn't simply about more schmoozing; this is a call for you to explore genuine, mutually beneficial insights that will give clients new ways to think about their problems. This includes delivering value with referral sources and strategic partners in ways that benefit your best clients as well as your partners, and building platforms that provide clients with anything they need to meet their objectives.

Today's sales superstars attract, teach, convert, serve, measure, and, most important, *guide* their clients and prospects while developing an individual brand that stands for trust and expertise.

The chapters that follow in part I cover the mind-sets, typically rooted in marketing, that sellers must now adopt in order to compete and thrive in business.

CHAPTER 1

Listen Perceptively

If speaking is silver, then listening is gold.

—Turkish proverb

E ffective salespeople have always been good listeners, keeping an ear open for opportunity. Given our society's information overload, the need to listen well has evolved exponentially, requiring salespeople not only to use the ability to monitor and filter what is being said, shared, written, and reviewed, but to identify what an opportunity looks and sounds like in an increasingly chaotic environment. Today's salespeople must develop listening skills and employ monitoring tools that allow them to stay in tune and add insight to the information shared by clients, prospects, and competitors alike.

Relearning Listening

Most people are born with the ability to hear and, over time, to interpret what they're hearing. Somewhere along the line, though, we become so unconsciously competent at hearing that we no longer feel the need to listen. You've surely heard someone call another person "hard of hearing." Well, most of us become "hard of listening" before our hearing ever begins to weaken.

Many books on sales cover the topic of listening, and in particular, active listening, but I believe there is a form of listening beyond active listening that requires more skill—and returns even more value.

The ability to listen *perceptively* to what our prospects, customers, staff, and community members are saying allows us to more fully and accurately appreciate what they need. I believe we all have to work at developing our ability to listen perceptively.

So, What Is Perceptive Listening?

People who teach this sort of thing will tell you that there are many forms of listening.

Passive listening: when you act as though you are listening to a prospect, but are instead just waiting for your turn to speak.

Selective listening: when you are discussing a problem with a prospect in hopes of finding an opening to pitch yourself.

Active listening: when you are listening carefully to someone and reacting primarily to the words being said.

Perceptive listening: when you hear and interpret the words as they're said, but also consider what the person isn't saying, what she might really be thinking, and how she is acting as she speaks.

Perceptive listening is by far the most complex of the four because it requires you to be totally focused, completely mindful, and, well, perceptive of the conversation—about what is spoken and what remains unspoken.

Perceptive listening reveals things that a distracted or even mostly active conversation can't reveal.

Perceptive listening will tell you that when a prospect says he's not ready to buy, what he is *really* saying is that he doesn't understand the benefits of what you're offering.

Perceptive listening is how you draw out what prospects or customers are truly passionate about. It allows you to understand their goals and objectives, voiced and unsaid, and helps you map out a way to help them manage and then move toward achieving those goals.

The party being listened to can actually sense when you're listening perceptively. We've all grown pretty numb to the act of conversing with people who divide their attention between our words and their iPhones. When someone is fully focused on our words, attitude, frame of mind, and even posture and body language, we're sensitive to that kind of attention.

I believe you can even use perceptive listening to monitor the things you say to yourself. When you are mindful enough to stop and witness your own thoughts and perceive how they truly make you feel, your actions will be much more perceptive.

This kind of effective listening can be learned, but it takes practice. It's a habit of sorts, just like multitasking is a habit. The more often you actively engage in perceptive listening, the more easily you can tap into this mind-set.

Below are three exercises I challenge you to undertake in an effort to build your level of perceptive listening. Let's bring this art front and center in everything you do.

I. LISTENING TO A CLIENT

Make a list of five clients you respect and would like to understand better. Schedule a time to get together with each of them, in person if possible, and ask the following three questions. Give their answers your full focus and pay close attention to how they answer—notice their word choice and body language. (Obviously you'll have to adapt this a bit for a phone interview.)

- What's the one thing you love about what our company does?
- If you referred us to a friend, what would you say about us?
- What's the biggest challenge you face in your business right now?

2. LISTENING TO A TEAM MEMBER

This time, set a time to speak with someone you work with or with whom you have a professional relationship that you would like to develop further. Ask him the following questions.

- What's the one thing you love most about coming to work here?
- If you referred our company to a friend, what would you say?
- What's the biggest challenge you have in meeting your goals right now?

3. LISTENING TO YOURSELF

This might be the toughest act yet. Sit down and pose these questions to yourself. Pay attention to how you feel about the answers. You aren't looking for right or wrong answers here, but be honest. You're merely checking for cracks in the alignment.

- What's the one thing you love most about what you do?
- Why do you really do what you do?
- If you could do anything you wanted, would this be it?

Listen with Your Body

Let me ask a seemingly odd question: How good do you think you would be at selling if you lost your hearing?

Before I go any further with this idea, I recommend that you listen to a brief TED talk by Evelyn Glennie called "How to Truly Listen." (You can find it here: http://www.ted.com/talks/evelyn_glennie_shows_how_to_listen.html.) In this inspiring presentation, deaf percussionist Glennie illustrates how listening to music involves much more than simply letting sound waves hit your eardrums. Glennie lost nearly all of her hearing by the time she was twelve, but still chose to become a composer and percussionist. As she explains in her talk, not being able to hear has given her a unique connection to her music.

Glennie is able to make music because she can listen truly—and in a way most of us wouldn't even think about: she listens perceptively. Likewise, we need to think outside of the belief that listening to the sounds in a conversation—what's being said—provides its only worth. It's time to dig beyond that, into what is being portrayed in our own bodies and in those of our clients and prospects.

Pay attention to how your client is moving, where you place your eyes when you speak, and how you model someone's posture. All of these factors are an essential part of listening perceptively and ensuring a client feels heard. Even paying attention to your own breathing as you listen to a client allows you stay more focused on the intricacies of the conversation. This doesn't have to be a distraction; simply take note of the state of your breathing. I find that all too often we are so focused on what we're going to say next, we don't relax and hear what the other person is saying. Paying attention to your breath is key to relaxing and really hearing.

As long as I'm stretching you here, let me give you another powerful way to experience the practice of perceptive listening. How about taking a ballroom dancing lesson? There is perhaps no greater way to learn to listen to another person using all your senses than dancing with her. You have to listen to and interpret the beat and tempo of the music, and remember whether you are leading or following. Dancing requires you to respond to the subtlest movements and "directions" while also trying to remember the next step. Every part of this communication is carried out wordlessly—yet if you're a perceptive listener, you'll still know exactly what to do, without words!

Questions Are a Listening Device

Good questions always trump even your best answers.

When speaking with a client or prospect, sellers need to take a cue from marketers and utilize the power of questions. Instead of pitching your idea, strategically ask questions to figure out what it is your customer needs, or is concerned about, or wants to see from you. Sometimes you have to pose question after question to get at what the problem actually is. In many cases, a good line of hard questions can help identify and eliminate a problem a client thinks he or she is trying to solve. Marketers know that good questioning can reveal a lot.

The Socratic method, named after the classical Greek philosopher Socrates, is a form of inquiry and debate between individuals with opposing viewpoints based on asking and answering questions to stimulate critical thinking and illuminate ideas.

In some ways a sales call is a form of inquiry and debate between individuals that starts with opposing viewpoints. Through proper questioning and listening, you can move the conversation in the direction of common ground.

The Socratic method is widely taught in law schools and in training psychologists, but it certainly has a place in the repertoire of the sales guide as well. But beware: I've seen some sales trainers teach the Socratic method as a form of planned inquiry that's robotic and downright manipulative. This turns off savvy buyers. Asking good questions is an intentional, yet subtle, art. The goal must be the progress of the idea on both sides, not just one person trying to win over the other to his side of the table.

Asking the right questions is the key to get you and the client to the right place together. There's nothing less fruitful than a salesperson spending thirty minutes answering the wrong question because the right one hasn't yet surfaced. Questions create clarity and get your prospect to open up in ways that reveal how you can add value to the relationship.

The best consultants ask great questions instead of trying to provide great answers. It's a valuable service in and of itself and demonstrates that you are there to guide your client toward his or her objectives rather than close a sale.

Asking tough questions can take some nerve, but if you're in front of the right kind of prospect, she will respect you for caring enough about her success and satisfaction to make the extra effort. That goodwill will get you to a better relationship much faster—even if a closed sale is still a ways down the road.

Your Question Workbench

As you get better at asking questions, you'll also become a better listener and help your clients articulate their needs in ways that your competitors cannot.

Try to have the following questions ready in every sales situation. The right question, posed at the right time, can demonstrate that you truly understand the challenge or that you can quickly get a sales presentation back on track—or it may simply allow you to check in on how a prospect is feeling.

Can we get specific? One of the most important things you can do is to figure out what clients really want to know when they ask a question. Often they don't know how to be specific. So they might say, "Tell me about your products," when they really want to know if you test your products against a specific defect that they discovered in their current supplier's product.

Be prepared to redirect a broad line of questioning to get more detail. Ask "Can we get specific? Is there anything particular you would like to know about our products?" You can always move away from this stance, but more often than not, the person you're questioning will answer in a way that helps you understand what's going on in his worldview.

Is there a specific question? Have you ever had a prospect ramble on about what's wrong with everything in her company (and perhaps the world as a whole), only to then stop and ask you to solve it? The challenge with trying to sell in this situation is that it's a lot like trying to wade through a pond without any idea how deep the water is. Try flipping the script back to the prospect or client by posing a question like "What specifically would you like me to address?" It's the only way you're going to get her to focus on the matter at hand. Instead of trying to frame your answer in response to a giant problem, ask her to break it down for you.

Why is that a problem? Again, many times people will tell you all about what they perceive as their problem without shedding any light on what it's costing them or why they want to solve it. Your job is to see if they can articulate the situation for you. If they aren't motivated by this question, or can't answer it clearly, they won't be motivated or ready to solve it either.

What does that mean? The moment prospects start throwing around clichés and industry buzzwords, call them out by asking them to explain that jargon in layman's terms. If they're using the word "synergy," for example, ask "What would synergy look like in this case?" This will force the client or prospect to clarify his understanding of the language he's using and actually link it to his own business. Further, if you truly don't understand something a prospect is explaining, ask him to go deeper. Most people love to explain what they do and you'll look good for listening closely enough to actually know when to ask these questions.

How do you measure success? Often, a salesperson is out selling a product or a solution on the basis that it's good for the prospect, but without knowing how the prospect is measuring what's good for her. When you understand what a buyer's objectives are and how they are measured, you can frame your value in those terms. This is a tricky one as sometimes it's not that obvious. Many times, a buyer is mostly concerned with the things that show up on his annual review, and you'll benefit from understanding that.

Let's say your software can save frontline folks over forty minutes a day and you know that could add up to substantial savings on labor costs. But your prospect isn't that worried about labor cost savings because his big goal this year is to increase employee satisfaction. Do you think that might be useful to know?

What is the purchasing process in your organization? Probably the most important line of questioning, in many situations, centers on the buying process. Your prospect may not have the ability to reveal all of the layers and hoops, but you had better understand what her role is as a buyer, especially if she is part of a larger organization.

How does that make you feel? If you get your prospects to reveal how they feel about a problem or a potential opportunity, you then hold a measure of emotional control in a sales situation. At the very least, this question will allow you to gauge the importance of the situation. If they don't seem to be too concerned with a solution, for example, they may not be as far along in the buying process. However, if they react strongly— with anger, or fear—to a certain problem, that's a clear sign that your value will come in by helping them figure out a useful solution quickly.

What would you do if this were solved? Problems and challenges take people away from the things they are much more excited about. Figuring out what a potential buyer would rather do than solve a given problem gives you some insight into what's important to him or her.

What do you enjoy most about your business?: I find that many business owners and even corporate managers started out doing what they love, then lost sight of it along the way. Helping them remember what they love about what they do and setting a course back to it can be a great service. No one else is asking prospects this, but it's a great way to make a connection.

How would you spend your time if . . .? This is the kind of question that would often come later in a selling or service situation, but I think it can be useful to find out, in an active way, what someone is interested in doing in his spare time. People really appreciate someone genuinely inquiring about the things they may even have stopped asking themselves.

What would 10 times X look like? Often, customers don't think as much as they should about the big picture. Get good at helping them look at problems in much different ways by suggesting they think more broadly about them, or that they think in terms of the challenges they would face if, instead of simply trying to meet their stated objective by 10 percent, they thought about what it would take to double that, or triple it—or more.

When you get a prospect to think much bigger, you can get her excited about a future result and address other challenges and constraints she may not yet be thinking about. This is the place where you can take charge of defining the new problem.

Why is now the right time? There are many reasons to figure out why someone is inquiring about what you have to offer right now. You may uncover some hidden pain or simply unmask his real motivation. Are his needs tied to a particular business cycle? If you can unveil the time line of his buying process, you will have a better understanding of where you stand in that cycle.

What didn't I ask? I've found that you can ask lots of clarifying questions and still miss something a client really wanted you to ask. Give them the chance to lay it on you. I can't tell you how many times information extremely relevant to the situation comes to light from this question.

What did we agree to today? Always confirm commitments of any kind at the end of every meeting. Will you be scheduling a new meeting with them, or sending over a proposal based on today's conversation? If you agree to send a proposal, do some initial fact-finding or forward some research as soon as you get back to the office. Of course you'll want to restate any commitment the prospect makes as well.

You won't use all of these questions all the time, but you need to have them ready for situations that are variable and likely to change. Great questioning skills and the ability to interpret the answers reveal the core difference between a top sales guide and an ordinary one.

Start with one or two questions that help you get started in almost any situation. Play with them, get comfortable, and then add some more.

Listening Online

Finally, I want to focus on a somewhat new set of listening tools and skills—those enabled by technology and social networks.

It used to be that a salesman would gather intelligence by reading industry journals, asking clients about their environment, or simply by sitting in a prospect's office, scanning the walls for things like diplomas, family photos, and sports memorabilia.

Today, this kind of information—and a great deal more—is available online and through social media participation. An entirely new category of research tools and services has given the perceptive listener incredible advantages.

Listening for buying signals and signs of disruption allows sellers to create opportunity and to educate themselves about an industry. In order to do this, you must create a "digital listening station" and use it as an essential tool in your sales playbook.

There are five key types of online listening that will enable you to take full advantage of the wealth of useful data spilled daily into the digital world:

Listening for Connections

I wrote this chapter during a week's stay on the island of Saint Martin. As people are in the habit of doing these days, I snapped a few shots of the ocean and beach and shared them on Facebook. Immediately, several of my customers shared memories of similar trips and offered recommendations of restaurants on the island. Thanks to my posting and their responding, we now have that bit of connection in common.

Social networks make it very easy and acceptable to share everyday personal details about what we love doing, how we spend our time, and about activities and organizations we may support. This information is fertile ground for establishing deeper connection with your customers and prospects alike. Following, "friending," and adding your customers to a small Google+ circle is a must if you want to sift for nuggets of genuine common ground (but please avoid using the knowledge you gain in ways that are too personal or disingenuous).

To listen for connections, try tapping social networks and tagging your customers in your organization's CRM system. I provide further information on how to listen well online at the end of this chapter.

Listening for Buying Signals

Prospective buyers often talk about what's working, what's not working, and what's downright broken online, sometimes long before they start looking for help. Your listening station can help get you in front of a buyer before the RFP (request for proposal) process is even under way. Pay attention to what your customers are posting on Facebook or tweeting—what they're complaining about, what they're praising, and whom they're engaging with, including your competitors.

Another great benefit of mining social networks is that you can find out who reports to whom, how people measure success, whom they currently work with, and perhaps how they like to connect and buy. You can learn a lot about people's perceptions of the buying process by perceptively listening to the signals they send online.

You might also want to take the time to create a group of your hottest prospects and add them to a Twitter list or CRM tool that allows you to easily scan what they are talking about and sharing in social media.

Listening for Changes

Most sales reps have learned that change is neither inherently good nor bad; how you see it depends on your current perspective. For an entrenched supplier, change might spell a reopening of the selling process. For someone on the outside, it might spell a great invitation to begin a new relationship.

Monitoring networks for change is a great tool. You can keep tabs on your current customers and spot potential for moving in on new opportunities. New hires, new product launches, and acquisitions are the kinds of changes you'll want to keep tabs on; they can spell opportunity in the right situations.

Listening to Stay Informed

Your listening station should also include resources that allow you to easily plug into your customers' world or, where you may not possess deep knowledge, to become informed about the challenges facing industries. It's not just about listening to what your prospects and customers are saying; it means listening to what *they're* listening to. Know what blogs they follow, what magazines they read, what conferences they attend so you can understand what they're getting through other channels.

This is also the place to focus on listening to your competitors for signs of weakness, changing directions, and opening doors. What a competitor's current customer is sharing in social networks can be very telling as well.

Listening to Add Value

We all know that the wealth of information and data available these days can create information overload. That's not great, especially if you don't know how to manage it. But if you do, you can take the data overload as an opportunity to sort out the clutter.

Aggregating and filtering information is a way for sales guides to add value to their prospects and clients. Those who master digital listening will start to use their strategies to help their clients sort through the noise and focus on the information they really need.

Filtering out the chaos and presenting good, useful information to your clients and prospects is another great way to use listening as a way to differentiate yourself; the practice allows you to offer listening and filtering tools to your clients as a part of your service.

Tools and Tips for Perceptive Listening Online

The following list of tips and tools should help you build a fairly robust setup for just about every kind of digital listening, described above:

- Use Signals from HubSpot to track a variety of buying signals.
- Create a Twitter list of customers and track it in HootSuite or TweetDeck.

- Add the Rapportive social browser plug-in to track social activity in Gmail.
- Use social CRM add-ons for tools, such as Salesforce or Nimble.
- Create Google Alerts for your best clients.
- Subscribe to the blog feeds of your best clients by using Feedly.
- Use a tool like SproutSocial for monitoring, listening, and engaging.
- "Friend" customers on Facebook.
- "Fan" prospects' Facebook pages and monitor them in HootSuite.
- Subscribe to a sales intelligence service such as InsideView.
- Monitor prospect industries in services such as Trackur.
- Set up industry folder groups of top blogs found in Alltop.com.
- Subscribe to industry topics in Q&A sites such as Quora.
- Find industry leaders on Twitter by using Twellow.
- Create industry influencer circles in Google+.
- Make Twitter lists of influencers by industry (Twitlistmanager is a nice tool for this).
- Follow industry news sites such as MarketWatch.
- Invite industry leaders to share one or two insights via e-mail.
- Use content curation tools such as Scoop.it to build category-specific pages by industry.

CHAPTER 2

Connect the Community

In traditional selling, a great deal of energy was focused on the prospect, the potential customer who was most likely to buy your product or service. Today, you must focus not only on the prospects themselves, but also on the larger community that surrounds an organization.

"Community" is a broad and often misunderstood term as it applies to business today. I submit that the highest objective of any business is to build a vibrant community. For our purposes, I specifically intend "community" to include the entire ecosystem that surrounds a business—customers, employees, suppliers, mentors, advisers, and users of all kinds.

Community has a great deal to do with a business's ultimate success. By learning how decision makers function at every level, how a company's culture operates, and how community is formed within an organization, you can create greater value on behalf of that organization. This is an area that even marketers often overlook; by understanding it more fully, a salesperson can create a tremendous strategic advantage in the market.

The concept of mining and connecting community may seem like a foreign approach at first, but the fastest way to gain access to a prospect is through the portal of community. In this chapter, I'll outline how a vibrant community is built and how you can adopt the skill of "community anthropologist" to more effectively understand a prospective client organization or even an entire industry.

It's time for sales teams to take note and understand how community forms, how to gain access to community, and how to help prospects and customers form a better understanding of this all-important element—not because it's the trendy thing to do, but because it will change the way you gain access to them.

Why Community Matters

The idea of community in business has taken top billing in recent years, obviously due in large part to the growth of social networks and the communities they foster. Many organizations fortunate enough to have forward-thinking leadership and marketing departments have even added the title Community Manager to their organizational chart, usually under the VP of Marketing.

Selling has become far less about individual relationships and much more about aggregate relationship value. The days of being outgoing, telling jokes, and buying dinner to win business have given way to showing up with a value add over what a buyer can get on their own through a search engine. Decision makers don't need more traditional salespeople to meet their objectives; they need people and organizations that understand how to deliver value.

One of the best ways to deliver value is to understand organizations better than they understand themselves. To do this, you need to identify the individual players in their community's world and understand how the parts all fit together. Often, organizations don't understand all the ways they affect their community. That knowledge gap is an opportunity for a marketing-minded salesperson.

How Community Forms

Connecting the dots in an organization's community requires a deep understanding of how community forms in most businesses. It's not about Facebook pages and catchy marketing slogans. It's much more subtle, and requires that you start thinking about organizational elements that you've probably never considered in the past.

I've always liked the word "confluence." It's a word most commonly used to describe the point at which two rivers come together. My hometown,

Kansas City, was founded at the confluence of the Missouri and Kansas rivers. The image of these two powerful channels coming together to form something even more potent is the perfect metaphor for how communities prosper and grow.

I believe that community forms around a business through six elements. What I would now like to propose are six genuine community driver opportunities for a salesperson to mine.

When analyzing a prospect or an existing customer, you should dig into each of these six drivers and formulate initial determinations about how they might affect your approach to a new (or existing) client. Each driver is accompanied by a process you can use to uncover clues that will help you build value in your sales process. This is where some of your newly acquired listening skills will come in handy, showing you how to home in on activity in each driver.

In effect, I'm asking you to do a fast audit of your prospect's marketing and organizational effectiveness. This may seem a bit odd at first, but once you master a few steps, you'll be able to size up a business and quickly gain potent insights into what the prospect cares about, how to effectively approach her, and how to engage her community.

The ability to "deconstruct" a prospect's community—to analyze all of its aspects in order to gain insights into how it operates and how you can gain access as a trusted guide—is an invaluable skill. The first three drivers are decidedly internal, those that make up the community inside the business, predominately the staff or employees. The last three drivers help determine how a community experiences a business from an external point of view. External drivers are those that specifically affect customers, prospects, and users.

Clarity

I wrote extensively about clarity in a previous book, *The Commitment Engine*. What I discovered as I wrote it is that most organizations that foster loyal and engaged communities also have a single-minded, active purpose—a reason for why they exist. Quite often, what drives them has little to do with the products and services they offer. Clarity of purpose is a crucial starting point; it's the kindling that starts the community fire.

Tom and Mary Miller own a janitorial services company in Cincinnati, Ohio, called Jancoa. I shared their amazing story in my previous book because it illustrates the idea of clarity wonderfully.

The Millers found that their greatest challenge was their inability to retain enough people to complete the work they sold each month. To solve this problem, they dug into their employee pool to see if the problem was there—and discovered that the workforce attracted to the kind of work they had to offer had essentially lost all hope of achieving much for itself. Living in poverty and hopeless conditions had robbed these workers of their dreams.

The Millers decided to make their company's purpose about helping people recapture their dreams through a program they called the Dream Manager. Every employee was encouraged to identify and go after his or her dream—and their Dream Manager made sure they did.

Their company is now about making dreams come true, and it's changed everything about why people come to work there. It's the one true thing that anyone attempting to sell to them had better understand.

The company is successful not just because they offer good janitorial services, but because they—and their employees and community—have clarity of purpose. Janitorial work is the service, but their deeper purpose is making people's dreams come true. How many of you have this kind of clarity about your prospects' or clients' true reason for existing?

CLARITY ACTION STEPS

To understand an organization's purpose and see how they communicate that clarity to the community, go to the community. Locate a handful of customers and employees of the prospect you are targeting and plug them into a simple CRM to monitor their social media activity. It's amazing what you can learn about an organization by watching how they interact on sites like Facebook and Twitter.

Quite often you'll find evidence of what they stand for, what values they promote, and how they interact. Their actions online can tell you a great deal about who they are as an organization. You might also discover that their public words and actions aren't necessarily in alignment with their marketing messages.

If you can find a way to ask questions of their staff or customers, even better. You're looking for clues as to what the market really thinks of their brand. This is also a nice way to uncover some opportunities and unmet needs.

Culture

In many ways, culture is simply clarity amplified and acted upon. People who are attracted to the clarity of a company's purpose join the cause and strengthen it. Without a set of beliefs and corresponding guiding principles, clarity becomes vague; only through the existence of a culture that supports the purpose does clarity come alive in an organization.

Bill Witherspoon founded the Sky Factory to make, in his words, "a beautiful corporation" after he had failed to do so in the past. Before he ever bought a piece of equipment to use in the creation of the digital skylights the company installs, he went to work on designing a culture that would drive the company.

At the Sky Factory, everyone is an owner, everyone knows the numbers, everyone rotates through management functions, and everyone participates in major decisions. Their company culture dictates a great deal about how they buy, and understanding this allows a salesperson to approach them in a way that values that.

CULTURE ACTION STEPS

If you have any luck uncovering an organization's employees, you might simply watch for clues that tell you how they view working for the company. Twitter is actually a pretty good place to learn about company culture. You can watch the way a company interacts with its community and get a read from actual customers or users on how they are being treated. You'll probably succeed in finding telltale clues, and this can be a fruitful way to understand an organization more deeply than their website marketing-speak could ever reveal.

Research the company's written materials, their mission statements, core values, and the like. Do these seem to fall into line with some sort of higher purpose for the organization? Do they seem to align with their reason for existing? Can you think of a single word that the market might use to describe their brand?

Method

Communities don't generally form around products, services, or companies. They form around ideas, methodologies, and processes that allow them to have something in common with other people and communities.

Method is the catalyst for the energy required to gain momentum in the market and among a community.

To me, this suggests the vital importance of creating and communicating unique methods and points of view that help buyers figure out how to think about their problems in ways that no one else has. When you can do this, and you give your way of thinking a name and a set of steps, you create the potential for a shared language around an idea. By doing this, you've created fuel for a cause—and given your staff and your customers a way to evangelize in a common tongue.

David Allen, the author of *Getting Things Done* and the time management system of the same name (known by fans as GTD), readily admits that all he created was a simple method for time management—but it turned into a movement. His method spawned numerous tools, websites, and apps, all built by a community that had been empowered through a common language.

METHOD ACTION STEPS

A company's methods can often be found through a little digging into things like white papers, ebooks, and brochures. Does the company seem to rally around a unique point of view or way of doing business? Do they use and promote their own terminology, processes, and checklists? By monitoring a prospect's various forms of communication and mining their social networks, you may discover they have created a community of customers who can speak to one another using a common language.

Content

Content is essentially the story a company uses to communicate purpose, culture, trust, and method to the outside world. It's the tool that gives the community a growing voice (for good or ill) and how, over time an organization builds a body of content and knowledge that ultimately communicates a much bigger story.

In many ways, this is the point where the internal and external worlds of community collide. The various forms of content an organization puts out should help them tell the story of why they do what they do while also communicating in a way that educates, informs, builds trust, and ultimately moves a prospect toward becoming a customer.

Content is also one of the richest ways to engage community members. Do customers participate in creating content? Do they receive lots of feedback and comments from readers and users? Do employees at every level participate in the creation of content?

CONTENT ACTION STEPS

Start by building a library of every bit of content the prospects or clients put out. You can learn a great deal about what they value and where gaps exist by understanding an organization's approach to creating content.

Do they use content to build awareness, trust, and engagement, or employ it only when they try to sell? If possible, become a customer of the companies you're researching and see how they use content in the sales and follow-up processes. What do their e-mail responses to inquiries look and sound like? Is their content intentionally shareable?

Presence

There are many access points to a business and its offerings. Social media has certainly increased that access, and perhaps simultaneously diluted it by giving people so many choices for how to engage.

An organization's story must unfold in a total presence both online and offline. The company must open up access points in social networks, e-mail, advertising, and PR. They must create a culture of listening and responding. They must facilitate and collaborate at every turn. People now discover and join communities in ways that marketers never consider on paper.

You can tell a great deal about an organization by understanding how integrated their online and offline efforts are. How they choose to maintain their presence across different channels, and through different parts of their community, is very revealing.

PRESENCE ACTION STEPS

Collect as much advertising, public relations, social network, and referral activity on your prospects and clients as you can. Subscribe to e-mail newsletters and campaigns. Engage in social media contests and "asks."

Are they sending a clear and integrated message? Do elements occur that don't seem to go together? Does their marketing presence match the clarity and culture research you've done?

Touchpoints

In my book *The Referral Engine,* I introduced something I call the Marketing Hourglass. The power of the six drivers is lost if an organization doesn't create a logical plan to move members of the community to act, buy, and refer others.

The above framework helps engage and attract members to a community, but you still must draw the map that allows them to engage at the highest possible level. This is how you turn a community into a direct revenue stream, but it's also how you allow members to sort, sift through, and determine their roles. A community member who doesn't purchase can—and quite often does—influence others. By creating levels of engagement you allow your community members to define the roles that make sense in their world and cultivate the ecosystem needed to foster complete community.

The basic idea behind the Marketing Hourglass is that an organization creates intentional touchpoints that move people through seven stages: know, like, trust, try, buy, repeat, and refer.

TOUCHPOINT ACTION STEPS

Your job is to construct a map, using the Hourglass concept, of all the ways you see an organization engaging prospects and customers. The simplest approach to creating a touchpoint map is to first create a grid listing the steps—know, like, trust, try, buy, repeat, refer—down one side and then see if you can add all of the ways that your prospect comes into contact with his customers and prospects. Try to map out his sales process and customer service processes. Again, see if there's a way you can become a customer or community member by purchasing, subscribing, and attending events whenever possible.

The Community at Large

Now it's time to step back and analyze community from a bigger-picture standpoint. One of the best ways to really learn about a prospect's challenges is to not simply view them as the organization sees them or explains them, but view them from how the market or their community views them. That's the real point of this exercise and that's how you provide a completely different kind of insight in the sales process. If you can provide this kind of insight, you'll already be ahead in terms of offering a valuable point of view.

Start by identifying all the community members that play a part in a thriving business. Who are the key vendors, suppliers, and sponsors relative to your prospect? Who influences or mentors the management of this organization? What strategic relationships exist? Who are their referral champions?

By studying an organization's community in this manner, you can add value as a seller by helping the company connect to additional partners in new ways, ways that not only foster greater community, but also lead to greater sales.

For example, most businesses will tell you that they generate a significant amount of business by word of mouth, but they have no idea how to quantify it or measure its impact. Looking at an organization's larger community will offer some insight into how and why word of mouth builds and how to make it grow.

By understanding key strategic partners, you can gain access to even greater insights about how an organization works—and spot potential referral and partnering opportunities that exist in your own growing community and network.

Building Your Community

How might you apply what I've covered in this chapter to the creation of your own community? If you want to change the way a salesperson's role is perceived, you must change how you consider your own place in the business world.

To begin with, think about how you can build your own community. As an army of one, what's your position in relation to your customers, prospects, referrals, vendors, and others?

Building community doesn't have to run counter to anything your organization is asking you to do (in many cases it will only enhance your sales process). A vibrant community is the greatest asset any business can possess and it's the greatest asset any individual salesperson can possess.

So, how can you apply the elements of community—clarity, culture, method, content, presence, and touchpoints—to your own community-building efforts?

We'll turn to answering that question in the following chapters.

CHAPTER 3

Define Leads

Using your newly acquired knowledge of how to build and deconstruct a community, let's dig into the ways you can become a master at defining the kinds of leads that are perfect for you and your organization.

In a traditional model, an ideal sales lead was initially defined by the marketing department. Leads would then be funneled into the marketing pipeline and handed to a salesperson only at the appropriate time.

As a top sales guide, you have to understand how to define and attract ideal leads instead of waiting for the marketing department to hand them to you. By challenging the assumptions sent down by marketing and narrowly defining what makes an ideal lead, a sales professional can create processes for both finding and standing out with this narrow group. Lead defining can be done across demographics, but it is done most profitably when you can define an ideal prospect's particular behaviors.

For example, I know that a business owner who participates in industry or community associations and boards is much more likely to value investing in business improvement overall and is therefore much more likely to value the professional services I offer.

Too often, sales managers target a market segment by size or industry, tell them what they have to offer, maybe work in a little solution selling, and hope the prospect chooses them. Or they target a market segment, respond to RFPs, and hope the prospect chooses their price.

Either way, what's being built is a recipe for frustration, low prices, and even lower profits.

The problem with solution selling and responding to RFPs is that each approach basically makes every business look the same. When that's the case, price rather than value becomes the primary focus.

The secret to creating a consistently engaging sales process is to understand how to choose your clients, and not the other way around. Although it might sound counterintuitive, you need to select exactly whom you intend to work with and let your unique value add illustrate why working with you makes so much sense.

Now, when I say choose your clients, I don't mean you should make a list of clients you want to work with or that you think would be nice names in your prospecting list. What I'm referring to is the intentional act of identifying the characteristics of an ideal client and focusing your community-building efforts on prospects who fit that profile. Taking this approach allows you to significantly increase the likelihood that you will end up working with clients who appreciate your unique approach and insights.

Defining Your Ideal Customer

There's a pretty good chance that your marketing department has spent time uncovering target markets and studying demographics, psycho-graphics, and other measuring tools to define who and what makes an ideal customer. This strategy mostly implies that you determine in advance the makeup of a market that your business seems suited to attract.

The thing that's always bothered me about this approach is that it relies on the lowest common denominator: "Whom can we attract?" Instead, try thinking of your market from the opposite point of view. "Whom do I deserve to work with? What qualities would my ideal customers have?"

I've spent years evangelizing the idea of finding your ideal customer. I believe you deserve to work with customers who appreciate your unique value. For me, this mind-set focuses on prospect behavior as much as demographics.

Some might say that the idea of salespeople choosing their customers is somewhat egotistical—but it's not at all. If you want to work with the leaders in your marketplace, then you'd better up your game so that you deserve to do so. Defining your ideal customer, it turns out, is actually quite a humbling—and centering—idea.

I was talking about this very idea with a longtime friend, Eric Morgen-stern. His firm, Morningstar Communications, has experienced tremen-dous success and his roster of clients reads like a "most desired" list. Eric listened to my thoughts on finding the ideal customer during my presen-tation to a group of business owners and shared with me how behavior plays an extremely large part in the clients Morningstar Communica-tions seeks out—and, just as important, doesn't seek out.

According to Eric, they look for clients that are "nice, smart, and suc-cessful. Two out of three is not sustainable."

They've identified the behaviors that make up an ideal client. Morn-ingstar looks for companies that are "involved in the community," as they tend to value effective communications and a high level of service, "lifelong learners" in that they tend to value effective communication, and true leaders who believe that "an educated customer is a great cus-tomer."

Eric added: "So much [of figuring out who your ideal customer is] is a gut feeling about the organization and its leadership, based on expertise and experience."

In order to figure out who your ideal customer is, I recommend that you sit down with your marketing department and start talking about the behavior, traits, and distinctive qualities of customers you know and want. Begin by exploring the types of clients that you don't want to work with; knowing whom you don't want to work with can be as illuminating as knowing whom you want to engage.

A client of mine did this exercise for his design and consulting busi-ness. He and his team made sketches of the kinds of clients they did not want to work with in such a way that it was much easier to define what the ideal looked like. They created fleshed-out customer personas, with names like Lottery Winners and Destined to Be Small to frame qualities of red-flag customers. They even went as far as identifying existing cus-tomers they no longer wanted to work with.

That's the funny thing about identifying ideal customers: until you know whom you'd choose to work with, it's far too easy to take on custom-ers who drag you away from the work you deserve to be doing.

Saying it doesn't make it so, but until you are able to define, under-stand, and nurture the customers you truly deserve to be working with, success will elude you.

Again, my belief is that this is where listening to and deconstructing community will pay off handsomely. When you start to pay attention to the players, competitors, prospects, and leaders in your industry, you start to gather some pretty great insights into why one customer makes a far greater partner than another.

Behavior Matters

Once you identify the larger pool of prospects—those companies that match the size of the company you target, as well as the industry, the right structure, and the right software—it's time to turn your attention to a narrower subset of prospects who have demonstrated behavior that reveals their willingness to respond to your unique approach.

Let me give you an example that might apply to any service-oriented business.

I discovered long ago that there are three categories of behavior that stand out as crucial markers for an ideal client. It almost doesn't matter what industry they appear in. If one of these three characteristics is present, I can charge ahead with confidence, knowing that I want to work with that client.

Movers: Movers are people who care about their industry almost as much as they do about their business. They have a need to serve and they realize that by improving the overall health or impression of their industry, their company wins.

These people often serve on industry and association trade group boards and committees. They're always looking for ways to improve their business.

Educators: Educators teach as an approach to selling and business development. They hold classes, create useful content, and often are found leading discussions and presentations both related and unrelated to their core business.

Not surprisingly, this behavior model responds very well to a teaching-oriented, content-based educational approach.

Skeptics: This last group might seem odd, but I've discovered that skeptics can be as open as anyone else to new approaches to their business and industry. Often, what they've grown skeptical of is everyone saying the same thing, while no one is actually delivering results.

Sometimes the only way to uncover skeptics is through networking, but this group may also be open to a disruptive approach. Have you ever attended a networking event and spoken with a prospect about an issue his company was facing and who, in the same conversation, revealed all the ways that problem could not be fixed, including the solution you happened to sell? That's your skeptic.

Set some time aside to analyze your current customers in the light of these categories. Are there any common behaviors they share that you want to look for in ideal customers? Do your best customers hire lots of consultants, attend training programs, participate in industry associations, value teamwork, and invest in their people? Perhaps these are the kinds of behaviors you might find in your most ideal customers.

Use your listening skills with your current customers to identify behavior cues. And by all means, get together with your marketing department to brainstorm about ideal customers. By reading this book, applying these ideas, and taking what you've learned to your sales and marketing departments you'll likely increase your value within the organization—and help your organization focus their energies on customers who deserve your attention.

Triggers Matter

As I mentioned in chapter one, you should create listening routines specifically geared to picking up what I call "trigger phrases," the kinds of things you know your most suited customers are always saying. The listening stations are a key to identifying an ideal customer. To look for triggers, try the following tools:

- Set up alerts for industry, competition, and customer changes.
- Follow LinkedIn notifications to spot job changes.
- Track announcements that signal changes in personnel or strategy (key new hires or new product rollouts).
- Be prepared to jump on changes that play into your organization's unique skills, such as technology changes and earnings announcements.

This approach puts you on alert in ways that make you more valuable to your existing customers. Tune your listening for triggers that might be useful for your customers. Imagine how much more value you could demonstrate by opening doors for them or pointing to an industry trend or change they could seize. Can you make referrals and recommendations based on something you heard about a client's industry? Being able to no-tify your customers about trigger events before they spot them can make you more than just another salesperson in their eyes. You can add value to that relationship by relaying information you're already listening to.

What triggers exist in your industry?

Create Personas

It's pretty easy to get caught up in marketing-speak when it comes to customers and to start thinking in terms of target markets and market share and the like. Remember, though, that in the end even the buyer in the big corporate purchasing department is a person.

The next practice I recommend is defining and sketching the makeup and personality of your ideal customer—creating a persona. This is some-thing that smart marketing departments have done for years.

The term "persona" originates in the theater world, but it translates wonderfully to the world of business, where character development, story lines, and emotional connection are staples as well. I love the term; it draws heavily on personality traits and behavior, two of the most impor-tant elements of a good fit between seller and buyer.

For marketers, a persona takes the form of a detailed sketch of exactly what an ideal customer looks and acts like. This prototype customer is described and talked about as though he or she is a real person, maybe even given a character name like Mary or a descriptive title like Techie, as well as an image. The key to creating and using personas is that Mary and Techie's behavior must be described in a way that gives clues as to what they expect, and how to spot these clues.

In my world of marketing consulting you might meet a persona named Bob, the learning-focused business owner. Bob owns a software business and loves to learn; he soaks up everything he can and knows where to find more. Bob reads books, attends online seminars, and can spout the latest business lingo. He researches thoroughly before he makes a deci-sion and relies heavily on information from his network to do so. He craves a combination of coaching, teaching, and do-it-yourself ap-proaches to building his business and demands the right to dive deeper into subjects on his own. Bob wants help on things he does not under-stand and validation on the things he is working on to make sure he is on the right course.

Because I know Bob's persona, I can map out his behavior and needs more deliberately than if I were flying blind. Accurately creating customer personas takes some practice, but there are some things that we can keep in mind in developing them for any industry.

Adele Revella, president of Buyer Persona Institute and author of *The Buyer Persona Manifesto,* describes what she calls *Five Rings of Insight* that are required to accurately create customer personas.

1. Priority initiatives—What's important to your customers right now?
2. Success factors—What would success look like to them?
3. Perceived barrier—What might hold them back from buying?
4. Buying process—How do they gather information and make a purchase?
5. Decision criteria—How do they come to a decision?

Revella's work is focused primarily on large organizations, but these considerations work for any size business. As you consider this notion of defining and creating your own ideal customer personas, give some thought to how each of these five considerations fits into that persona. They can shed light on why (and when) a customer may or may not work with your organization.

Discovering and using customer personas combines the gut feeling from your own experience, your analysis of current clients and prospects, and consideration of Revella's Five Rings to ask your customers and prospects why they do what they do. Developing a set of personas—highlighting characteristics you and your business are built to attract—will help you attract the right kinds of clients.

My friends over at HubSpot have created a handy template that you might want to download and use as a guide to creating personas: www .offers.hubspot.com/free-template-creating-buyer-personas.

Add Social Signals

Smart sales guides, as I've mentioned, have already discovered the awesome power of mining social networks for leads. This practice is very similar to gold rush prospectors panning for gold with little more than an idea and some hard work staking their claims.

We've moved past the point of crude social-lead digging to a much more elegant phase of social interaction. Prospective clients are being discovered, scored, and nurtured using social networks and everyday relationship-building tools. In fact, the practice has become so accepted it now has several names: social selling and social-lead targeting.

As services such as LinkedIn, Facebook, and Twitter have grown in importance, so too have the tools that mine the rich set of sales data found in every interaction. But the big breakthrough in social selling oc-curred, in my opinion, when tools that mined social data started com-municating with one another.

No longer do we need the mammoth do-everything-in-one-enterprise type tools to compete. A lone salesperson armed with HootSuite and Nimble accounts, and about twenty dollars a month, can become a social-lead-targeting ninja.

Now, I'm not saying that some of those more expensive (and more complicated) tools aren't awesome. If you work for an organization with the budget, full-time IT support, and someone to pull the levers and adjust the mirrors, such tools can be a wonderful source of information.

But if that's not you, let me ask you this: Would it be helpful if you could easily find people on Twitter who are searching for the products you sell? Well, anybody with a little Twitter search mojo has been able to do that for years now, but what if you could also

- Instantly know everything those people are doing on other social networks?
- Find out who your leads are, who they are connected to, and how to contact them in several channels?
- Easily create a contact record that unifies all your communica-tion with them?
- Track what they do on your website and see how they react to your e-mails?

You can easily do all of this and more with little or no tech support and very little overhead. Don't you think this could make you a better sales-person?

So far I've only mentioned Twitter, but with the right tool setup and integration, Facebook, LinkedIn, and Google+ can be used for the same kind of discovery and targeting.

Building targeted lists is only one way to look at what I'm talking about. You can also build a connected network of your customers, share targeted insights, and facilitate engagement and partnerships better when you adopt this kind of targeting mind-set.

The key piece of the puzzle is integration, and these days there are plenty of powerful programs that integrate information easily and almost seamlessly. (I go into more depth about using high-tech tools in upcoming chapters.)

You can easily build a list in Twitter based on your ideal persona characteristics and some search criteria. Then with one click, you can add selected list members to the Nimble CRM tool for a complete picture of the prospect, along with unified messaging. So, now if you reach out to that prospect by way of a subtle connection tweet based on a stated need or request, Nimble captures your entire conversation, shows you the prospect's social stream, and reveals her key connections all in one screen.

Social engagement is not so much a channel as it is a behavior that allows for much richer listening, targeting, nurturing, learning, and converting. The key is to bake social data and signals into your entire prospecting and sales process using the tools that put this vital set of data at your fingertips. The real skill then becomes using this information to add value!

Ideal Prospect Profile

I've thrown a great many ideas at you in this chapter as a way to get you to think beyond the traditional sales process in defining leads. Let's recap and then together build a tool that you can use immediately to collect some of the most important elements of your ideal prospect profile.

Create a one-page Word document per persona and include the following elements:

- Persona name
- What makes him or her an ideal customer?
- Key behavior
- Key objectives
- Key motivation
- Key barriers

- Buying process
- What a great result looks like

Use this tool as your checklist for spotting ideal opportunities and as a way to educate potential referral sources and strategic partners. Think of this tool as your answer to the question: "How would I spot my ideal customer?"

Now that you've developed your ideal-customer descriptions, we can switch gears to focus on how you'll go about attracting and communicating with more prospects who fit these profiles.

CHAPTER 4

Find Your Value Proposition

Markets are often very attracted to companies that stand for something greater than a group of products. Sales guides can benefit from connecting their own passion and purpose to that of their companies and using those qualities as part of their story. Knowing your own value proposition and combining that clarity with your organization's promise is how you create leverage in a highly competitive sales environment.

The process of standing out by delivering greater value starts with understanding your unique ability and how you can use it to guarantee real results. In some ways, this step aligns with the clarity element we discussed in chapter two. However, you'll need to be clear about what you do that makes a difference. It's all about identifying your X factor and using it to add value for your clients.

Find Your Personal Value Proposition

Value propositions are sales and marketing staples. It's very difficult to start a purchasing conversation unless the potential buyer understands how the product or service he is considering adds value in a way that sets it apart from other offerings.

Can a salesperson create a value proposition or unique ability to add value? I think they most certainly can. One of the keys to standing out in a competitive sales landscape is to discover, then communicate and amplify, your greatest strength as your individual value proposition. If you lack a strong value proposition, you can be sure that you'll land in the prospect's "no" pile.

Every organization must provide value, first and foremost, through its offerings, but as a buyer considers options, the individual salesperson's value proposition, reputation, process, and brand can play a big role in the final buying decision. These factors certainly play an important role in customer loyalty in the long run.

How you sell is just as important as what you sell, and who you are dictates your best way to teach, advise, and sell.

The first step in figuring out how to utilize your value add is to gain a better understanding of your personal strengths and the impact you have on the people with whom you interact. Simply considering this concept, and identifying your strengths and offerings, will make you a better salesperson in every circumstance.

There are two other useful tools that can help you determine your value proposition. The first is the work of my friend Sally Hogshead. In her bestselling book *Fascinate*, Sally introduces the Fascination Advantage, a scientifically derived personal brand assessment she developed with the team at Fascinate, Inc., which incorporated test results from 125,000 participants. This test will reveal how your personality adds distinct value. The Fascination Advantage test uses twenty-eight assessment questions to determine which of the fourteen personality archetypes fits you best.

The second useful tool is the work and insight of the Kolbe Index, created by Kathy Kolbe, a leading expert in cognitive development and assessment. The Kolbe A Index measures a person's instinctive method of operation (MO) and identifies the ways in which he or she will be most productive.

Both Kolbe and Hogshead focus on helping people discover their unique abilities and value propositions. They seek to help you use the strengths you already have in a way that benefits everyone around you, as opposed to trying to shore up your weaknesses.

Many personality tests measure how you see the world, but these two help you understand how the world perceives you.

Perhaps you've taken personality tests in the past or have been told you have a certain makeup that's perfect for sales. I contend, however—and both of the above resources support this—that there is no right or wrong personality for sales. Sure, if your job calls for you to go out and cold-call all day, it helps to have a certain Teflon-like resilience. But if you understand that your job as a salesperson is to educate and bring insight in order to create a better process than your competitors, then knowing your core strength and figuring out how to use that to add value is the most important way to differentiate yourself in a meaningful manner.

I suggest that every business owner, entrepreneur, and salesperson take both the Kolbe Index and the Fascination Advantage assessments. Better yet, take these tests to your sales and marketing departments and have all the team members assess their personal brand strengths.

People who take these tests commonly note that they are very empowering. In some cases, simply knowing what your strengths truly are can clear up a great deal of confusion about the way you should work to be most effective.

Getting Customer Feedback

Once you've completed your own personality assessments, it's time to get some feedback from another extremely valuable source—your customers.

Remember those ideal customers we talked about in chapter three? I want you to select a handful of your existing customers who fit that profile and interview them.

A word before you begin: you're not looking for scientific data, you're looking for themes and stories that offer clues to what clients see as your unique approach or style. You're not asking them to validate that your service was good (it should be, if they stayed with you!); rather, you're looking to uncover patterns of where and how you add value.

Below are some useful questions to ask these ideal customers:

1. *Why did you buy from me in the first place?* Here you are looking for clues to what helped them decide to buy, what built trust, and what resonated with them in your marketing and sales processes.

2. *What's one thing I do in the sales process that you love the most?* Stick to discovering the one part of the sales process they like the most and help them get as specific about it as possible.

3. *What's one thing our organization does that others don't?* This may sound a lot like the second question, but what you are really trying to do is get some industry comparison going. Have you succeeded where in the past others have failed?

4. *If you were to refer me to a friend or colleague, what would you say?* This is your chance to have your customer describe what you do best, as though she were telling a friend. This point of view can be very powerful and the answer could turn into a testimonial. In many cases that's precisely what I've done with answers to this question.

5. *Can you tell me about three other companies that you love?* This question allows you to better understand what they think best-of-class looks like and why—and it helps you build a list of potential strategic partners.

6. Bonus: If you can pull this off, ask the customer you're interviewing to conduct an online search in front of you. He should imagine that you and your service were no longer around and he needed to replace you. What phrase would he search for? For example, someone looking for accounting software might search for online accounts receivable programs before looking at the broader accounting software.

Work with Themes That Matter

Based on your interviews, see if you spot rich, recurring themes in your customer's responses. What statements did you hear repeatedly? Maybe multiple customers told you they like how you don't talk down to them, or that they appreciate how quickly you call then back when they have a question.

Don't look at this as pure science; it is based more on gut feeling. Probe for stories, and ask customers to define what "better service" means to them. In many cases you will hear some of the same things over and over, so drill down into those themes and see if you can get to the essence of what your customers really value.

Don't underestimate the power of simplicity. Quite often you will find that your clients value the little things you do. Resist the temptation to

dismiss these as unimportant enough to use as your core point of difference. If your clients are telling you that something—your friendliness,
your ability to make them feel heard, your quick response time—is how
you add value and differentiate yourself, listen to them.

What I certainly hope you hear in these interviews with your ideal
clients are things such as

- You help us look at problems in a different way.
- You help us consider all the possible approaches.
- You're always sharing new ideas, tips, and tools.
- You help us know where potential land mines could be hidden.
- You teach us about trends that will affect our business in the
  future.
- You frequently challenge us to think bigger.
- You're more of a consultant than a salesperson.

If not, then we've got some work to do!

Now, do the answers you received mesh with the value proposition
used by your organization as a marketing tool? Does your organization
clearly communicate a powerful point of differentiation? Do your customers understand your organization's brand promise?

I realize that the answers to these questions, or the challenges they
present, may be outside of your ability to control. However, understanding how to align your personal brand, sales process, and value proposition with that of your organization, or finding ways to take your new
insights to a candid discussion with your sales manager and the marketing department, are key steps in becoming a sales superstar.

Your Talking Logo

For the last step in analyzing your customer interviews, I want you to
take the most potent bit of feedback you received and turn it into your
own personal sales affirmation. You can be as serious or as playful as you
like with this, but the idea is to create something that keeps you focused
on one of your core points of differentiation.

Craft your sales affirmation as your answer to the question, "What do
you do for a living?" Instead of instinctively responding, "I'm in sales,"
consider how your customers see you and the roles you fill. They don't
think of you just as a generic salesperson; you offer specific value. So your

sales affirmation might be "I help manufacturers look at problems in a different way" or "I challenge business owners to think bigger."

You may never actually utter these words to a real person, but I hope you see how creating what I call your "talking logo" might help you stay focused on consistently showing up with your core value proposition in mind on every sales call and during face-to-face sessions with your clients.

Your talking logo, much like an effective company logo, is your personal branding identity phrase.

The Number One Unmet Need

In addition to asking your clients to tell you what you do that's unique, you should consistently ask, probe, and dig for any needs that aren't being met—even those not directly served by what your organization has to offer. You've always got to be on the alert to discover what your customers can't get (or what problems they can't solve) and assess how badly they need a solution.

In order to be successful in sales in the long term, you need to be ready to solve the problems nobody else is solving—even if you don't yet know how to do that. Starting today, make it a habit to ask your customers some variation of the following five questions and look for patterns, unmet needs, and opportunities to change how you approach your business. Then, perhaps once or twice a year, go back to those customers and ask the questions again.

I credit former psychologist turned Internet marketer Dr. Glenn Livingston with developing the basis of these questions. Livingston uses sophisticated research techniques to uncover niche problems people are desperately seeking answers to. Then he uses this deep research to create information products, AdWords tactics, and sales copy that address these niche needs.

Unmet needs survey questions:

- What is the biggest challenge you are facing in your business?
- Why is it important that you find a solution to this challenge now?
- How hard have you worked to try to solve this challenge in the past?
- What is it about this challenge that makes it so hard to solve?
- How hard has it been to find an answer to your challenge?

Ultimately, you're looking for patterns of unmet needs that people are motivated to solve, but have had a very difficult time finding solutions to—even though they've looked long and hard.

This approach has powerful implications for sales. Every market has gaps of unmet needs and the salespersons who address and solve the hard problems can differentiate themselves and their company in ways that others won't even consider.

This path is the surest route to success, but it isn't the easy route. If your job is to find solutions to problems your customers don't necessarily know they have, don't expect to turn up quick and tidy opportunities to solve unmet needs.

Furthermore, the research you uncover from taking this approach may run seriously counter to your organization's business model, products, approach, and positioning. Be prepared to fight for some changes internally involving your marketing, R&D, and customer service departments based on what you learn.

The ability to differentiate really does determine your success. And the secret to unparalleled success is to differentiate by solving the greatest unmet needs of your customer.

You Versus Your Company

The way you differentiate yourself as a salesperson is as important as the way the company does.

Buyers have become so adept at doing initial purchase research that they no longer need or have the patience for a sales presentation on the benefits of your widget. Ironically, this applies doubly for B2B sales—where you might think a little face time on the sales of big-ticket items would be a good thing.

A Corporate Executive Board (CEB) study of more than fourteen hundred B2B customers across industries revealed that 57 percent of a typical purchase decision is made before a customer even talks to a supplier. So, in a majority of the cases a decision was made, based either on whom to invite to bid or whom to actually purchase from, before anyone knew the prospect was a prospect. This same CEB study also found that 53 percent of those surveyed claimed that the sales experience itself was one of the greatest contributing factors in continued loyalty to the brand.

What does this mean for the typical sales professional? It means you'd better find a way to make your sales approach as useful and distinct as the products and services you are selling. Sales is no longer only about being found and providing educational information (although those are still important). To stay relevant, you must have prospects looking to you as an adviser, teacher, time-saver, problem solver and guide on life's journey.

I repeat: it's not just your product or service that must perform, it's your sales and marketing process that must provide these things as well. Although most products, services, brands, and even pricing are about the same among various competitors, the sales experience—the value, ease, and insight delivered during the actual process of buying—tips the scale in favor of (or away from) your company.

There are three marketing-related books that hit this theme pretty hard: Mitch Joel's *CTRL ALT DEL,* Jay Baer's *Youtility,* and Matthew Dixon and Brent Adamson's *The Challenger Sale.* All three confirm that the sales and marketing process is the differential that keeps customers and prospects devoted to you.

Make Your Sales Process More Useful

Let's say you are shopping for running shoes. Your research finds a few sites that carry the selection you are looking for. A couple stand out by providing a lot of information on the shoes and featuring reviews from other runners. Still, you're not sure which $150 pair of shoes is right, and that's enough money that you want to get your choice right.

You fire off a couple of questions to sites that seem the most informative. One sends you shoe specs from the manufacturer. Then Patton Gleason from OptimalRun.com sends you a personal video highlighting all three pairs of shoes you were considering and telling you why, based on your needs, he suggests a particular pair.

Now, you tell me—is that sales process useful? I'd say so!

The beauty of this kind of sales process is that it greatly favors the company that understands and delivers on their value proposition, no matter the size of the organization.

Here's what some of Gleason's customers had to say:

- It was amazing and so helpful and kind: I finally felt like someone was actually listening to me instead of just trying to rush me into making a purchase.

- You're too great—this is awesome that you answer with a personal video.
- Thanks again so much for your help, it especially helps to be able to see the shoes other than just in photos.

Ladies and gentlemen, this is the new standard. Creating sales insight, follow-up, and consulting that's so useful people will be willing to pay to receive it.

CHAPTER 5

Build a Reputation

L et's face it: all things being equal, we prefer to do business with people we know, like, and trust. In today's online world, trust building means something entirely different than it once did, or, at the very least, it means something much more expansive.

Reputation and trust building used to be controlled, for the most part, by the folks back in marketing. But then a sea change occurred—the Internet and social media gave the customer a far greater voice in the way a company was viewed by the rest of the world, and how that view was communicated.

You must think in terms of building an online and offline reputation in much the same way an organization might think about creating a brand. When a prospect is considering a purchase, the sales representative's reputation for delivering value, as well as the social proof that bolsters that reputation, is increasingly crucial.

There Are No More Blind Dates

With a sea of potential information close at hand, there's really no such thing as a blind date anymore. If set up on a blind date today, the first thing that most people would do is turn to a search engine to learn all they could about their date's reputation.

The same is true in many marketing and sales environments. Not only are prospects digging online to find out about companies and products they're interested in, they are also researching the sales professionals who may be involved in the sales process. That's right—prospects can now know just about as much about you, personally, as you know about them.

And why not? If, as we've already discussed, the only real reason to involve a salesperson in the purchase of a product or service is to gain more knowledge and insight, isn't a little research to determine who has the best reputation for providing these things warranted?

The amount of research may depend greatly on the significance of the purchase and how involved a potential sales and service staff might be in the decision process and delivery of a result; but the reputation of a salesperson can be a key ingredient in winning or losing a deal.

The good news is that your reputation, both online and offline, is something you can and should proactively manage and amplify. Many organizations and sales professionals don't even consider this level of branding, but you should. Think about it this way: let's say you make ninety-nine successful sales and have one big, fat flop. The person on the other end of the flop or misstep—the unhappy customer—tweets, reviews, comments, and shares what she interprets as a major failure on your part and that of your company.

If you've done nothing to counter this one bad result, it rises to the top when someone searches your name. Even if your organization has done plenty to balance the good and the bad, if you're not vigilant your personal reputation can take a beating and cost you valuable opportunities.

These days, building a strong personal brand is a career move that every salesperson must take.

Claim Your Real Estate

To some degree, your personal brand or reputation offline is what clients and others who interact with you deem it to be. So never forget that even with all of the focus online, how people perceive and receive you offline is still vitally important.

Online, however, a great deal of your reputation is built through non-active interaction, such as information on profiles, social media activity and engagement, and even the number of followers you have on Twitter.

A great deal of this online participation just fills a space that a prospect now expects to see. It's not uncommon to include basic searches for reputation gaps as part of initial due diligence. It's actually become a bit of a red flag, in search-based research, to find little or no information about an individual or organization or, as mentioned previously, little to counterbalance one negative review.

To some extent, your online reputation is a numbers game. The first step toward building a solid presence is to establish and enhance a large number of social profiles. This enables you to build search results for your name; search engines will certainly index content from some of the larger players such as Facebook and LinkedIn.

In upcoming chapters, we'll go into detail on how you can leverage these networks and enhance your brand, expertise, and credibility. First, however, you need to wade in and start creating your individual presence.

While some organizations worry that individual branding in social networks can lead to confusion, I contend that organizations gain a great deal when their individual salespeople are active in a smart way and linking back to the organizations they work for.

Dan Schawbel, a personal branding expert and author of *Promote Yourself: The New Rules for Career Success,* offers this advice for people trying to raise the stakes in their careers and establish personal brands that complement the organizations they are also a part of:

"Start your own website to centralize your work profile. You need a single place where you can store everything you accomplish and that should be a website under your name (yourfullname.com). By doing this, you can easily refer others to your work, whether it be hiring managers or for freelance projects. As you grow and develop your career, add new projects, education, skills, and examples of your work to your website. Your website is a living, breathing resume that is always available to people, even when you're asleep."

Creating a Powerful Bio

It's funny, but most salespeople don't think about their social profiles until they're looking for a new job. I'd like to suggest that you look to your social profiles as a key starting point in building a stronger digital footprint.

If you have not yet done so, claim a personal profile on Facebook, LinkedIn, Google+, and Twitter. If you have already done this, consider creating Pinterest, Instagram, Reddit, and Quora profiles as well.

You might also consider employing a service such KnowEm, which for a fee will claim your profile on a hundred or more social networks.

Another option is to submit your name to the service BrandYourself, which offers tips on how to get the profiles that actually represent you—not someone else with your name—to have a better chance of showing up on page one of searches. Regardless of which service you choose to use, claiming your own personal name on as many networks as possible should be your first priority.

A Good Social Profile Starts with a Good Photo

Once you've claimed the profile, add some detail to it. Don't just leave it up there with a generic image or no profile photo at all—and don't settle for that phone "selfie" shot, either! Get a series of professional shots done. It doesn't have to be a stiff studio shot; you can add some character, mix in outdoor shots, experiment with industrial backdrops. Just make sure the photo is well lighted and composed.

The dating industry has lots of data on the impact a profile picture makes when it comes to first impressions. While you're not looking for a mate, first impressions matter for your business life, too, and these findings can offer some instruction on best practices for profile pictures.

The dating site OKCupid cataloged over seven thousand profile shots and correlated these profiles with the number of contacts received. While they discovered some obvious dos and don'ts in profile images, they also discovered that a simple change in facial attitude correlated with as much as a 30 percent increase in contacts.

Women were approached more when they smiled, facing the camera, with a friendly and flirty attitude. Men, on the other hand, were more successful if they were not smiling and didn't look directly into the camera. Anything overtly flirty in the male photo was a definite no.

How do these online dating service findings translate to the world of business? While an overtly flirty attitude certainly shouldn't have a place in professional settings, the findings demonstrate that first impressions, particularly online, are driven by the profile photo.

When you first put down your footprint online, you may also want to check out services such as Vizify and About.me that allow you to build your pages by drawing from your social media participation and images you may already have online. These sites can also aid your overall search engine optimization (SEO) by giving you another piece of real estate—your branding elements and messages.

Resist the Urge to Cut and Paste Your Resume

Unless you've created a really engaging resume—experience tells me most sellers haven't—don't feature the same boring data in your online profiles that appear on your paper resume. Tell stories instead. Focus on where you've been, what experience you've gained, what skills you've mastered, and why. Write in the first person and use an active and expressive tone. Don't forget—you want to make your value add obvious, right up front.

Some of the best online profiles don't list job titles right after a person's name. Which of these two profiles would pique your interest?

A) John Jantsch. Marketing consultant, speaker, and author
B) John Jantsch. I help you make marketing simple, effective, and affordable

Jill Rowley, sales trainer and leading voice in the world of social selling, coaches salespeople to build "buyer-centric" LinkedIn profiles. No longer should your tagline say something like "quota crusher" or "expert negotiator." Optimize the line so that the buyer understands the specific value you bring to the business conversation.

Go back and revisit the talking logo you created in chapter two and use it as the subheading for your profile. Add a few highly relevant quotes from customers and employers that bolster your expertise and value proposition. Think back to the customer interviews I asked you to do in chapter three. These can turn into great opportunities to gather specific quotes about what you bring to customer engagements that helps you stand out.

Also, don't be afraid to talk about your passions in your profile, even if they are outside of your obvious professional requirements. If you've climbed Mount Everest, I want to hear about it.

I love this example from the opening paragraph of the LinkedIn profile for Jon Schram, CEO of a tech company called the Purple Guys.

"I love running! After kids, around the neighborhood, in marathons, and a business! As a husband, father, and business owner, I have many opportunities to 'run' things. A favorite saying is 'It's not how fast you run, it's where you're going that counts.' The Purple Guys keeps me busy during the week and family rules the weekends. Need advice on how to handle your IT hassles or how to juggle life and business? Call me!"

And by all means, link to your company website, to useful content you've created, and to all of the other social networks you participate in.

Lead with Your One True Difference

Although you need to start out by setting up profiles to cement your on-line presence, remember that building and maintaining a meaningful reputation actually requires some work. But before you explore the more expansive method of personal branding that will truly serve as an effective community-attracting and community-building mechanism, you need to narrow down your one true thing.

Your brand—your reputation for offering expertise and insight—must spring from the one true thing you stand for. This one deliverable becomes a story that you can transform into a greater narrative that will live on in your community

Instead of sharing everything you've ever done for your clients, and the many ways you add value, try telling fewer stories—but tell those few over and over again. Clarifying the one true thing you stand for can be used as a filter for reputation building, voice, and message.

You do this by:

- Narrowing your focus to an ideal client's unmet needs
- Sharing stories that build trust and expose vulnerability
- Helping define problems your customers don't know they have
- Giving your customers a way to collaborate and personalize
- Helping determine the real intent of your prospective clients

In her book *Selling with Noble Purpose,* Lisa Earle McLeod explains why salespeople who truly understand how they make a difference to customers outperform their more quota-driven counterparts. The research McLeod used as the basis for her work found that salespeople who sold with some sense of a higher purpose—who truly wanted to make a difference to customers—consistently outsold the salespeople who focused on sales goals and money.

Have you developed your purpose story? The thing that drives you to truly want to make a difference for your customers? I figured out my true purpose, though it surprised me. Here's how that happened.

The interior of the grand jury hearing room was anything but grand. It consisted of a handful of plastic chairs arranged in a way that must have made the jurists feel more like an audience than a court-appointed arm of the U.S. Department of Justice. I distinctly remember the lights. Maybe it was just me, but they seemed awfully bright.

What could I possibly have to offer as a witness in a hearing convened to possibly bring federal charges against one of my clients? As it turned out, I was a very boring witness with nothing to offer, but it was a turning point in my business—and perhaps my life. It was the point at which I defined the noble purpose for my business.

In an effort to build my business I had taken on a client who I knew was doing things I couldn't support, things that ran counter to my own values. As it turns out I was right, and the owner of this business was sent to jail.

In that moment of testimony before the grand jury, I knew that I would never again do business with a customer I didn't respect.

While this might seem like a rude way to find purpose, it's a story I often share as I define how committed I am to helping small-business owners, marketers, and sales professionals make choices that allow them to grow their business in ways that serve their higher purpose.

My one true thing found *me*. Now I often lead with this story in social profiles and presentations.

Develop Consistent Sharing Habits

Once you create these profiles, you've got to show up and weigh in on a regular basis.

In an upcoming chapter, we are going to roll out a plan for building your own content platform so that you'll have plenty to share and amplify in social networks. Before we do that, though, we need to set a foundation of participation and engagement. One of the best ways to do this is to make a habit of sharing.

Building on the advice in chapter one to create a listening station, I suggest that you now create a list of blogs to follow. Using a tool like Feedly or Feedbin, subscribe to the blogs of your competitors, your major customers, industry-related sites, and a handful of key journalists who might call upon you as a source for quotes.

In addition, add the blogs of noncompeting strategic partners to your list. Think of businesses related to your business, or perhaps even other salespeople from noncompeting businesses. Shoot for including perhaps twenty-five to thirty blogs from this category to your list. These sites will compose your go-to resource for sharing content with your followers and customers.

The benefits of being seen as someone who finds, filters, and shares good content extend beyond just a relationship with your customers; sharing other people's content is a crucial element of networking online these days. By consistently sharing the content from your strategically chosen list of blogs, you may begin to benefit from the same in return. You can enhance this tactic by also becoming a regular, relevant participant on a few well-chosen blogs.

To aid in your sharing efforts, I suggest adding a service called Buffer. Buffer allows you to select a handful of blog posts you might like to share and then "buffers" them out over the course of the day, so that you don't flood your stream by posting them all at once. Social media management tools such as HootSuite are also useful in scheduling and posting to multiple social networks.

Over time, make it a habit to share ten to twelve pieces of content every day. This is a big part of how you start to establish a reputation for sharing quality insights and developing a network of followers and fans.

Finally, consider working with a tool like RebelMouse, which aggregates all of your sharing activity to a single page on the RebelMouse network. This way all of your tweets, pins, and shares can be seen and consumed conveniently in one place. You can easily share this page with customers and other members of your sharing network.

Thoroughly Research Your Competitors

As long as we're focused on reputation building, now might be a good time to think about how your competitors approach this idea. You can learn a great deal about how to position your business and your personal brand if you understand the strengths, weaknesses, and strategic approaches of the salespeople you might come up against in selling situations.

Experience tells me that most salespeople don't know much at all about what their biggest competitors are up to when it comes to marketing and sales efforts. But setting up a competitor-specific listening station can uncover some useful insights.

Competitive research matters. First, you might very well learn that your competitors are doing little and that simply upping your inbound marketing efforts could pay immediate dividends. By thoroughly keeping tabs on the competition, you could gain a valuable understanding of their weaknesses and arm yourself with information that could help you determine messages that amplify your particular strengths as they relate to areas of your competitors' weaknesses.

In following your competitors, you might also learn—as I've seen countless times—that everyone in your industry is basically doing and saying the same thing. Use this wake-up call to find and communicate something truly unique.

Finally, you may pick up some tremendous ideas about how to make your business better and more effective by borrowing bits and pieces of your competitors' tactics.

Your Competitive Research Plan

Use some or all of these ideas to build your competitive listening station and track your competition more efficiently:

- Set up alerts in services such as Mention or Talkwalker to track the names of companies and individuals you compete with.
- Create lists to monitor their social activity on Twitter, LinkedIn, Google+, and Facebook and spend a little time researching their brand on SocialMention.
- Using a tool such as SharedCount or Topsy, do some research on what content is drawing shares and links.
- Subscribe to competitors' blogs using tools like Feedly or Feedbin.
- Get on every one of their e-mail lists. Use tools such as IFTTT to automate your research by storing competitors' e-mail campaigns to Dropbox or Evernote for easy retrieval and analysis.
- Download all published ebooks, research papers, and white papers. Use Google Advanced Search to find all the PDFs on their domain. Do this search to find them—file type: PDF [competitor domain].
- Enroll in all content series, events, and webinars.
- Find and follow competitors' YouTube channels.
- Find and follow their SlideShare decks.

- Subscribe to their Yelp RSS feed as a way to monitor their reviews.
- Research their pay-per-click advertising using a tool such as SpyFu.
- Study their SEO efforts using tools like Moz's Open Site Explorer or SEMrush to find out who links to their sites and what phrases are optimized for in each search.
- Find out where their executives speak and what conferences they attend.

When you automate as much of the above list as possible, you then simply do an occasional deep-dive analysis and occasionally check in to keep up to date on any new opportunities.

Networking: It's Not a Numbers Game

Before salespeople had social networks and other online tools, a great deal of their reputation was tied to effective networking. Every salesperson knows that effective networking—diving into circles of influence and creating profitable relationships—is how you get ahead.

The reality is that you can make social networking pay the way you've always made networking pay, by focusing on two things: whom you can help and who can help you.

If you accept that the basic networking statement above is true, you may also come to the realization that networking is not a numbers game. If you limit your networking to those you can help or target, and network with someone who can help you, you've got a real capacity problem, because in order to do either (or both) you must actually get to know something about the hopes, dreams, and goals of the person you're trying to network with—and you can't do that with a "follow" or a "like."

The surest way to make social networking pay is to build deeper relationships with fewer people. "Likes" and followers and witty tweets may create awareness for your brand and open doors for actual networking, but nothing can deliver the payoff of actually helping someone else get what they want or connecting with someone who can help you get what you want.

Here's the really interesting thing about this point of view. You both help people get what they want and connect with those who can help you get what you want in exactly the same way—through giving.

Here's a two-part assignment that can help you network effectively.

1. Identify five people you know you can help and who would appreciate your help. Reach out and offer to do something very specific to help them. Your only goal here is to raise these people up and to start a relationship with them based on giving.
2. Identify five people you know can help you achieve an objective this year. Reach out and offer to do something very specific to help them. Your only goal with this step is to become a resource for these people and to start a relationship based on giving.

Find out if they have any pet projects, new initiatives, or know of events that you can get involved in. Your primary purpose is to build an authentic relationship based on giving *first* and see what develops from that.

Sure, all that helping people get what they want might cut into making more cold calls, but by building fewer, deeper, stronger relationships you can make your social networking efforts and reputation pay off royally in the long run.

CHAPTER 6

Guide the Sales Journey

The concept of the sales and marketing funnel—getting lots of leads in the top part of the funnel and then narrowing down to work a few through the end—is so limiting in today's sales environment that we need to replace it with something far more representative of the whole picture, or what I like to call the real customer journey.

You have to find ways to inject your presence in a helpful manner into as many parts of the journey as possible. I believe that a sale isn't a sale until the customer gets an amazing result. If you realized your success was tied to this idea, would that change your sales process? Wouldn't that require you to think about what happens before an appointment ever occurs, after the yes, after the delivery, and after the fact? I think so.

Instead of seeing the sales process as a funnel—and your role as working leads or forcing buyers through that funnel—try instead to imagine yourself guiding your prospects on a journey. Specifically, you're guiding them through a set of seven logical buying stages—know, like, trust, try, buy, repeat, and refer. I call this the Marketing Hourglass.

When marketing processes are designed to guide prospects logically down this more expansive path, future lead generation becomes the natural outcome of a happy customer.

Certain steps in this customer journey have traditionally fallen outside the realm of the sales function—but the mentality that sales isn't responsible for building and protecting the process must change. As a salesperson, you must understand how all the pieces go together—marketing, sales, and service—and own every step of the process.

Understanding the Marketing Hourglass

Every selling situation and certainly almost every company will have a different approach to using the Hourglass framework. To get a feel for this concept, however, let's explore how a typical B2B organization and their sales team would approach the seven steps in the Hourglass.

We will cover many of the tactics mentioned below in greater detail in upcoming chapters. For now, I want you to see the flow of the entire approach as one idea.

Here's what the Hourglass steps and framework look like:

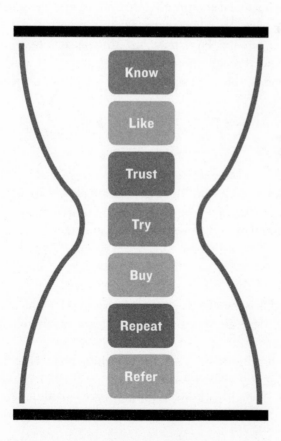

Know

This is the act of creating awareness. While it sometimes starts with a referral or through an introduction made at a networking event, it's often the act of putting something out there that gets the attention of your prospect.

Like

In this step you must move toward gaining permission to continue a conversation. Many times, the key here is to fire up your e-mail capture activities.

Trust

In this step you are subtly moving toward gaining the trust that comes from educating and demonstrating that you have something of value to bring to the table. Trust is perhaps the most important step and yet it's not one you can simply manufacture through one or two tactics—it comes together through a number of things.

Quite often in the next stages—try and buy—sales actively steps into the journey.

Try

The try phase is an attempt to get the prospect to sample what it might be like to work with your firm. This can be accomplished through a low-cost version of a product, analysis, use case study, or trial period. The try step is omitted by many in their desire to leap rather than lead.

Buy

Obviously, this is the step we all want, but in the Hourglass approach it's just another stepping stone to the ultimate goal—a thoroughly thrilled customer.

In some organizations this is the branching point. Customer service might step in here to close a sale or marketing might reengage to follow up or, worse, nobody really owns the journey from this point on.

Repeat

For most businesses, and for that matter most sales quotas, long-term momentum only occurs when existing customers continue to purchase over and over again as new customers are added. This step must be intentional, and designed at the beginning as opposed to being left to chance.

Refer

The goal of this system is to get 100 percent referrals from your client base. While it won't ever happen no matter how good you are, if you begin with this goal in mind, it's more likely that a higher percentage of clients will refer.

My goal in sharing this marketing approach is to emphasize that most organizations have gaping holes in their version of the journey. In order to think like a marketer, you must understand marketing as surely as you do sales in order to fill these gaps before, during, and after the sale.

In chapter eleven we'll take up the Hourglass approach once again as we talk about how to create and integrate the Sales Hourglass into your organization's marketing process.

Understanding the Customer Journey

Let's look at the idea of the customer journey in another, more expansive way.

As you consider any new initiative, campaign, product launch, or addition of content, answer these questions. You'll need to internalize this "complete customer journey" point of view before you start developing your approach.

I. **How will prospects learn about our value proposition?**

Your primary job is to understand and communicate, at every possible turn, just how your business is different from every other one that says they do what you do. As you plan for sales opportunities, you must know this value proposition inside out and be able to chart all the ways you will get it in front of ideal prospects.

This typically takes the form of advertising, networking, public relations, referrals, and strategic partnerships.

2. What will make my prospect want to know more?

To build the kind of trust you need to turn a lead into a purchase, it's not enough for your marketing department simply to create and run an ad. As a seller, you must build or tap into an education pipeline that your prospect can explore to learn how you are different and how you can make a difference for him. This kind of research can't be outbound. Your prospects must be able to find content on their own time, through what we might refer to as "inbound" research.

This step is often achieved through a content platform built on blog posts and ebooks and found on content networks such as YouTube and SlideShare and through interaction in social networks.

3. Why will our prospects give us permission to share our story?

This question really gets to the heart of the trust issue every business faces. The right to come to the table, to tell your story, is earned. Often, this is also the point in the buying journey where your reputation comes into play. Prospects who have come to this point are interested in what you do. Now, they need to learn how you do it in a way that corresponds with their values and beliefs.

Reputation management, reviews, SEO, content, and customer stories can make or break this element.

4. How will we offer proof that prospects will get the results they desire?

It's not enough simply to make a promise these days. Every prospect does his or her homework, so examples of broken promises show up as tangible proof of your business's mistakes just as surely as the copy on your marketing brochure tries to refute it. You must offer substantial proof that you can and have delivered a result for someone else. Case studies and customer testimonials are a great place to start, but nothing beats a real-life experience.

This is the place where proof of concept, trial offers, evaluations, workshops, or even freemium versions of what you do allow people to sample your ability to deliver. Offering proof in a lower-risk form makes it easier for your prospect to decide to undertake a complete purchase of your product or service.

5. How can we make the buying experience fun, effective, and convenient?

Once someone says yes, your job as the salesperson is far from over. At this stage, your focus needs to be on ensuring that the experience they receive is just as good at the treatment they received in the sales and marketing phase of the relationship.

Implementing a project or servicing the customer is crucial and, as a salesperson, you can't let this stage of the relationship slip through your fingers. If you want a customer for life, you have to consider selling to them for life. I know that the actual servicing of a client or product may likely be another department's responsibility, but if you let go of this part of the relationship, you'll only be called upon later to fix something that may be beyond repair.

One of the best ways to smooth any initial transition is through a formal new-customer orientation process that provides information and communicates proper expectations. Sometimes telling your customer what's going to happen and whom they need to know is a great relief. Make sure you insert yourself in making introductions to other key players in your organization and in meeting the key people inside theirs. At this stage, for example, you could ask your CEO to write to your customer's CEO to thank him or her.

Adding something special or surprising to this part of the sales process can go a long way to cementing your reputation and assuring the client that you're still thinking of her and her concerns. Buying your service team a gourmet pizza lunch is a gesture they won't soon forget. It's incredible how often attention to this question leads to referrals and word-of-mouth buzz.

6. **What should we measure to ensure that our customers get the results they expect and more?**

Sometimes, through no fault of the sales department, a customer doesn't get the result he had hoped for. There can be many reasons for this, but whatever the case, building a process for measuring your customer's results is one way to address problems before they turn into disasters—or begin to erode your credibility bit by bit.

A formal or informal results review process can uncover and address any lingering issues. Review also allows you to celebrate the value your solution or product brings to most customers and to use that proof, validation, and posture in future selling situations.

When you start to experience firsthand that what you sell returns to you (at ten and twenty times the cost), you can start having meaningful conversations about results and value that move beyond what the marketing department might be feeding you today.

7. **What will lead a customer to talk about us to his or her friends, neighbors, and colleagues?**

Exploring this question is one of the best ways to improve your sales. You should begin every client relationship with a referral in mind. Be ready for those moments when you know the prospect or client will be open to being asked about referral; and keep in mind additional touchpoints where you can plant the seed for referrals.

One of the best opportunities to plant the seed for referral comes when you're explaining to your prospects the result you intend to create for them. Tell all your prospects you're positive they are going to be so thrilled with the work your organization does that they will want to tell others how they can receive this valuable experience as well. Then create a process that ensures they will actually be thrilled, and collect those referrals.

When you begin to see that your role as a salesperson is similar to that of a guide on a long journey, you'll be better prepared to think in terms of your impact on the customer before, during, and after the sale. With this mind-set, you'll be on your way to creating customers for life.

CHAPTER 7

Teaching Sells

Imagine you're a buyer at a cabinet manufacturer, looking to partner with a new company for shop maintenance supplies. Several salespeople have reached out to you, offering their services. You have your choice of two qualified salespeople, both of whom provided good proposals.

Which sales professional would you choose, based on a random Google search: the one with a nice LinkedIn profile or the one who has published authoritative and expert ebooks, articles, and blog posts on the very challenge you hope to address?

Teaching sells today. You must attract leads, community, and opportunities by publishing educational content. While some marketing departments and sales managers might object to this idea, salespeople often have great insight into the world and the challenges facing the clients they serve and can raise their clients' level of perceived value and expertise by addressing their problems through blogging, curating content, and speaking.

The Inbound Content System

For the last few years, marketers have been using the term "inbound" to describe a major shift in buyer behavior. With so many ways to block out unwanted messages, traditional outbound marketing, and sales efforts, smart marketers have turned strongly toward an approach that is more about being found than about going out and hunting for new clients.

The primary tool of the inbound marketer is content—content that creates awareness, builds trust, enhances engagement, and educates.

Content has now reached the status of an obligatory marketing tool. Ironically, because it's everywhere, it's actually become less useful, almost generic, in the eyes of the overburdened buyer.

This is why a successful sales guide must enter the world of inbound marketing to bring some sense and insight to the overwhelmed buyer. To make a clear distinction here, I believe the individual salesperson is better equipped to personalize content in a way that adds value than a simple (and probably impersonal) addition of volume.

Unfortunately, a large percentage of the world still views the role of sales and selling as mostly outbound. This is why we still have sales managers who promote cold-calling and the use of telemarketing firms.

The fact is, if you believe anything you've read so far in this book, you must already realize that sales has become an inbound game as well. The cornerstone of this shift is the need for individual sales professionals to create content that attracts opportunities over and above—but hopefully in chorus with—the efforts of the marketing department.

What Exactly Is Content?

Content is multifaceted; it has several levels of definition and utility, as outlined below.

Content Is an Expectation

Today's prospects fully expect to be able to turn to a search engine or social network and find answers, or at least a data set, to address every challenge, problem, or need they encounter.

They also fully expect to find a rich fountain of content specific to the organizations and products they consider to be the solution to these challenges. They've grown to expect the selling company, as well as customers, networks, partners, and the media, to provide this content.

The logical extension of this view is that the in-the-trenches salesperson is the one who can best provide content.

Content Creates Awareness

In many cases, a prospect's first exposure to an organization comes not from a slick sixty-second ad but from an obscure blog post on a very specific topic of interest found through a series of search engine inquiries.

Building a library of content that reaches into these all-but-hidden corners of search is the essence of inbound marketing. This assignment should be the concern and focus of salespeople. After all, individual sales professionals are better equipped than anyone else in an organization to talk about the customer journey.

Content Builds Trust

In the inbound world, trust is pretty much everything. Obviously, the endgame is that customers ultimately trust that the product, service, organization, or solution they seek will address their needs, but the first line of trust is content. Do they trust the content your organization produced? Has the organization made the complex simple through content? Demonstrated their expertise? Maintained their reputation online?

These are the questions marketing and sales must address as they address the building—or erosion—of trust.

Content Provides Proof

Ever since prospects learned that just about any claim an organization makes can be supported or contested with a simple search, businesses felt the need to build content that offers proof of their results.

Sales professionals often hear customer success stories in ways that get at the heart of what really matters. Therefore sales, and no other department in the organization, is the best source of this important form of content.

Content Serves

Content that teaches customers how to get more, fix problems, and find the answers to common challenges and functions has become a tool that must be planned and executed with great care.

Twitter, for example, has become a public-facing customer service tool (for good or ill) and with it comes an entirely new level of service-based content.

Content Is a Referral Tool

One of the biggest stumbling blocks to referrals is the lack of tangible tools to point to something other than a website or brochure.

With the right mind-set, a sales professional can use a popular educational ebook or seminar as a way to get introduced to a strategic partner's entire customer base.

With this expanded view of content, let's move to addressing how a salesperson might think about creating a content system that serves the categories we just covered.

Creating Content

If content is to take an elevated place in the sales function, then you must take a planned and practical approach to creating it, making it useful, and harmonizing it as an extension of the efforts of the marketing department.

It's likely that your marketing department people are up to their elbows in content. Therefore, any content that you produce independently must be an extension of that effort. If I've assumed too much about what your marketing department is focused on, then by all means you'll need to charge ahead to fill this obvious void on your own. Do let me warn you, however, that waking up every morning and deciding what you are going to write on your new blog is not scalable.

As a salesperson, you need to visualize any movement into the world of content creation as a big-picture play. Think of this effort in the same way an author or magazine publisher traditionally does. Think about your total body of work almost as though you were going to write a book. By this I mean you should think in terms of all of the important chapters or themes of content that might apply to your field of work and develop a plan to create a total content system that grows with each passing month.

Failure to take this view will simply make this idea overwhelming. Where do you hope to be in your sales career in six months, in a year? That's the view you must engage when it comes to content.

But know this: content that demonstrates your expertise, attracts leads, and builds your reputation is a sustainable, renewable asset. Once you've built it, it can serve you for years and continue to increase in worth.

Total Content System

To build a clearer picture of how you get into the inbound selling game, I'd like to introduce you to the Total Content System.

The Total Content System approach allows you to plan, delegate, curate, create, collaborate, repurpose, and generally get far more out of every piece of content you produce. Once you implement this system, it will build momentum with each passing month and then multiply in value for you and your organization.

The Total Content System overview looks like this:

- Create a list of monthly foundational content themes.
- Develop your content delivery platform.
- Align your content with core business objectives.

Foundational Content Themes

Through your own knowledge of client work, and by brainstorming with your marketing or sales team and looking back on the myriad customer inquiries and questions you've answered, develop a list of core content topics for the next year. Come up with at least twelve, and assign one topic to each month for the next twelve months.

In effect, in this step you are establishing topics that will serve as the foundation of your inbound content efforts.

I've found that the best way to find your core content topics is through keyword research. Many search engine optimization firms engage in keyword research as a way to identify the best way to build pages that attract interest for high-traffic searches. You can find information on the best techniques for doing this by simply looking for the term "keyword research" or by reading tutorials put out by organization like Moz.com, SearchEngineNews, or Wordtracker.

Each theme should announce a substantial topic, related to your business or industry, that's also related to important keyword search terms.

Don't be too broad or too narrow in your theme selection. For example, let's say your business is a fitness center that offers personal training to professionals. Rather than simply writing generic content about fitness trends or tips, break your content into important categories such as nutrition at work, weight loss, and recovery and fitness on the road. That way you can start to build a focus library of content to use in the most important sales areas.

Your final list of topics should be broad enough that you could imagine using it to create workshops, a series of articles, and numerous blog posts related to each one.

You can also designate trending terms that you would personally like to rank higher but that currently have little or no content that leads people to you on that theme either online or offline. So a salesperson for our fitness center might want to debunk the latest fad diets one by one, for example, to rank higher on searches for weight-loss scams.

I'll use my own organization as an example to help illustrate this point. My business and model may be significantly different from yours, but these examples will help you fill in the blanks.

My editorial themes for 2013 were as follows:

- January—Referral Marketing
- February—Coaching and Consulting
- March—Sales and Lead Conversion
- April—Online Integration
- May—Writing
- June—Strategic Partners
- July—Customer Experience
- August—Content Marketing
- September—High Tech, High Touch
- October—Growth Strategies
- November—Analytics and Conversion
- December—Personal Growth

These all are topics that I know my community is interested in learning more about. Furthermore, I personally have an interest in developing more content around these topics. Do you see how I might easily come up with plenty of specific articles and blog posts under each main topic?

With these themes mapped out, I can now go to work on lining up ideas, guests posts, customer stories, new research, and related resources which, taken together, might create a valuable bank of relevant content to work with and point to in my sales efforts.

By the way, this is not a one-and-done kind of effort. These are themes that you will return to over and over again throughout the year in an effort to build a substantial library of content.

As you read through the first few sections of this chapter, you may get the feeling that I want to turn you into a full-time writer. Trust me, there will be a time and place for creating your own content (see chapter eight for more on this). But my goal here is to address ways to use other people's content, get your customers involved in content creation, and take content that's already been created by your marketing department to generate referrals and additional opportunities for exposure. You don't need to became a full-time writer—yet. What's important is understanding the power of content and leveraging it to serve your own needs.

Other People's Content

One of the best services a salesperson can provide for prospects and customers these days is to filter through all the content that's being produced and collect only the best of the best to share.

You probably feel sometimes as if you're drowning in information. Your customers feel the same way. Why not become a source of relief for your customers and prospects? (Value is produced in many ways!)

Finding and sharing consistently high-quality, relevant content (and adding your own insight to it) is not just a great way to increase the volume of your own content, it's a solid strategy to build trust in the *value* of your content.

Frankly, people are leery of reading only one point of view—the marketing point of view—so if you can share balanced opinions and information from other (potentially unbiased) sources, you can go a long way toward upping your credibility with a prospect.

Here are a number of ways to add other people's content to your routine.

Cobrand a Popular Piece of Content

Many people produce great content in the form of downloadable white papers and ebooks. In some cases, they do this to attract newsletter subscribers and links, but quite often they do it because they know something about a topic and want to document their knowledge.

With just a little research, you can probably find a great ebook that someone in your network would love to get her hands on. Now, some people might simply link to this content. What if instead you approached the ebook author and asked permission to send his book out to your networks, with full credit to them—and with the addition of one small information page at the back about you or your company?

With this approach, and with the right topics and content, you could potentially build a library of content overnight. You'd also make a valuable connection with that ebook author, with future opportunities for cobranding.

The Google filetype operator allows you to find lots of potential candidates for cobranding on just about any topic you can imagine. If you want to find PDF documents and ebooks about Facebook for business, for example, you would type: Facebook for business file type:pdf. Google will then pull up PDF files related to Facebook for business. Conducting a search like this will help you find ebooks authored by someone who might be very interested in allowing you to share his content. You can do a similar search for most of your other content themes and quickly be on your way to building the first wave of your content system.

E-mail Newsletter Snacks

Publishing a weekly e-mail newsletter is a proven way to stay top-of-mind with your community. However, because you're competing for in-box space with the many other e-mails people receive every day, you can't settle for a generic offering. Your newsletter content must be consistently useful, relevant, and convenient.

One of the best ways to meet these qualifications is to produce high-quality content filtered from other sources and delivered in snack-sized bites. You can easily find five or six great articles and condense them into 100-word abstracts to run in your e-mail newsletter.

Using tools like AllTop, Feedly, Newsvine, and Popurls, you can easily locate and collect content related to topics of interest to your customers and prospects. In choosing newsletter snacks, you might want to locate local bloggers to write guest content and offer them strategic relationships as you fire up your content distribution machine.

I've been producing a weekly e-mail newsletter just about every week since 2002 and I've played with different formats, different kinds of content, and different ways to present information. Currently, my newsletter format is designed to offer several compelling article abstracts grouped under a set of topics that I believe my readers expect from me. I author about 50 percent of the content and then hand select a couple of related blog posts from blogs I read.

When I switched to this snack-sized, scannable format, I immediately noticed that response and engagement increased dramatically.

Curate Topics

In order to really make content curation pay, you'll need to add personal insight to others' content.

So many people look at curation or pointing to valuable content as something closer to republishing. Republishing content does have value, but narrowly targeting a very specific topic and becoming known as a trusted source of insight on that topic is how you take content curation to a new level.

Below are some of my favorite tools for creating curated online content magazines.

- Scoop.it—www.scoop.it
- Storify—storify.com
- Curation Station—curationstation.com

You can also use tools such as Delicious, Evernote, Pinterest, and Pearltrees to simply clip, bookmark, and organize for republication the content you find online.

The key to making curated content work is to spend the time adding your own view of why the content is good or important or wrong—or whatever view you take that makes the content more useful.

RSS to HTML

This technique is perhaps a bit more technical, but it also allows you the greatest control over how you publish and display content from others.

Just about all online content these days comes powered by RSS feeds, making it easy to convert whatever content you find to HTML code that can be displayed on any page.

For example, if you want to publish positive mentions of your company's products on a new page on your site, you can set up Google Alerts to receive notice whenever your firm is mentioned in any online posting.

When you receive the alert, you can click through to the page and, assuming it's something you want to publish to your site, bookmark the content using Pinboard with a tag like "ournews."

Pinboard then creates tag-based RSS feeds so that anything you tag with "ournews," for example, can be displayed in a specific RSS feed. This gives you total control over what you want to appear in the feed.

Once you create the feed, you can go to Feedburner or RSS to include, convert the feed to HTML code, and embed it on a page or in a widget to easily display the content from the feed wherever you choose.

I know this may sound quite technical, but it's not really that difficult. Once it is set up, anytime you bookmark a new item, the item will publish to the designated page.

Think about specific industries you target, or even specific customers. Could you create a page of information from all your blog reading and competitive listening that might be useful?

Ask Pointed Questions

Another great way to get others to create specific content for you is to ask many people to answer one very brief question—for example, "If you could recommend only one book to a new salesperson, what would it be?"

This can be a great way to collect lots of suggestions, opinions, and insights to support or start a topic of interest to your readers. The other powerful thing about this approach is that you can often get higher-profile contributors to participate if all you are asking them to do is answer one question or finish one statement.

Once you collect all of your answers, all you need to do is add context and analysis to the list of responses—and post.

You can also easily embed a survey tool such as 4Q Survey on your site that asks visitors to answer some questions before they exit the page. This can be a great way to find out what people can't find and what they want more information on.

Customer-Generated Content

Your customers are often better equipped to tell the real story of the benefits and results you offer than an army of writers in a marketing department. So why not engage them to do just that?

Imagine taking your best, most loyal, most vocal customer along on your next sales call and asking her to briefly explain the real benefits of the work you've done for her. I imagine this would be very powerful. That's what customer-generated content does when it's done right—and that's why you need to routinely find ways to acquire it.

Below are a handful of specific ideas to help you get more customer-generated content.

One question testimonial—Create a survey that asks every customer one question, such as "On a scale of 1 to 10, how likely is it that you would refer us?"

Next, set the survey up so that if the answer falls between 1 and 4, the survey taker is redirected to a page that apologizes for his dissatisfaction and lets him know that he will hear from someone immediately to find out what went wrong.

If customers score you between 5 and 7 on the referral scale, they should be sent to a page that tells them that you're not happy until they are happier with their current level of service and asks them to suggest how you could have done better.

For the 8 to 10 scores, redirect the respondents to a form that allows them to submit a testimonial and asks them to check a box if they would agree to be interviewed for a case study.

This is a great way to automate testimonial generation and keep a real-time pulse on how you're doing. Tools like Wufoo and Formstack make it easy to run this process.

Video appreciation party—Once a year, hold a client appreciation event to say thanks to clients and prospects and allow them to network with one another and with your company.

Hire a video crew for the event. Create a fun, casual atmosphere at the party and at some point ask some of your clients to talk on camera about their experience working with you and your firm. Then, also let them record a five-minute commercial for their own use.

This is a great way to get lots of testimonials and case studies in one take. You'll find that your clients will often be very engaged in swapping stories and selling one another on the benefits of working with you.

Tell us your story—Getting your customers to share their experiences is a very powerful form of content. As an active salesperson you can probably interview your customers directly to extract this kind of content, or you can employ a handful of tools that makes it very easy to capture their stories.

For audio-only content, a testimonial recording line is a great way to go. AudioAcrobat provides a very easy system: you simply give your customers a phone number they can call to record their story. The service then produces an MP3 and a code to embed on your site that allows people to play the recordings.

You can also utilize a tool such as HireVue or MailVu that sends a link with a video capture tool to your client. Using a webcam, they can record a video testimonial or story and submit it—with little work on your part or theirs.

Community knowledge base—What if you could find a way to get your best customers to willingly shoulder the responsibility for identifying best practices and responding to your questions automatically? Tools like Zendesk, Help Scout and Get Satisfaction make it easy to enable community members to provide help and archived advice to other customers and prospects.

Robin Robins, founder of Technology Marketing Toolkit in Nashville, Tennessee, involves her customer community in her business in an incredible way. She has created a membership program that allows her IT business customers to receive ongoing business-building support through the coaching, training, and tools she provides.

To up the level of engagement, Robins has created what she calls "accountability groups" in the membership program. Customers head up these groups and do a great deal of work keeping fellow participants engaged and on track. Heading up a group is not a paid position; loyal and committed customers who want to play a bigger role in the community do it for free.

Help your peers—Using tools like Google+ Hangouts, Skype video conferencing, and GoToMeeting HD Video Conferencing, you can easily host and facilitate a group video conference for your customers and their peers to discuss important industry and business challenges and trends. You can record and archive the event and easily create useful and engaging content.

This is not a sales event per se, but by virtue of the fact that you have included customers in the conversation, there will be the inevitable discussions about what you've done to help them address a challenge.

Content as a Referral Tool

Hopefully, you do good work and people want to refer you to others on their own. That's the truth, but, hey, we're all busy and sometimes we need a nudge, a reminder, or even a tangible way to easily make referrals that make sense.

This entire chapter is dedicated to salespeople getting into the inbound selling game by producing content. Here's the really great news—content not only helps people find you and buy from you, it's also one of the best tools you can have when it comes to establishing strategic referral relationships.

Everyone needs content. If you can be the person who brings content to the relationship-building table, guess what? You win!

Content is an incredible tool for attracting a potent pool of strategic-partner relationships. Noncompeting businesses that also serve your ideal customer are valuable partners in this light. Your ability to share educational content would be a great way to benefit from one another's existing customer and prospect base and actually see referrals or partnerships emerge.

Below are a handful of ways to use content to enable vibrant referral relationships. (We'll talk more about each of these methods in an upcoming chapter, but for now it's important that you get the inbound-referral mind-set.)

Invited Content

Some people choose to categorize this referral as guest content, but if someone asks you to write a guest post on her blog or you ask someone to do the same on your blog, it's really invited content. So many content marketers try to force the idea of "guest" posts when in fact the best opportunities are earned.

Reaching out to potential strategic partners and offering them exposure on your blog or offering content in the form of a post for their readers is a great way to get referred and introduced to a strategic partner's community. This act also potentially lightens the content load for you and for your partner.

Cobranded content

If you or your marketing department have created a "must have" ebook to use in your lead generation and capture efforts (please tell me you have!), take that valuable content to potential and existing partners. Offer to let them send it to their community and even cobrand it with their contact details.

Your partners know they should be offering this kind of information, and because you showed up on their doorstep with a proven winner, they'll happily refer you by way of content.

This is a really great approach for a traditional supplier or service provider relationship too. Now your accountant or banker can logically introduce you to his other clients by providing something a bit more useful than a letter telling them how great you are.

Sponsored Content

One of the most powerful ways to utilize referrals is to be asked to present your expertise to a room full of your strategic partner's best clients. I call this approach sponsored content because the net result is that your partner sponsors the event and ushers you in front of an audience as a referred expert.

If you have a "must have" ebook, as suggested above, then you've got the makings of a "must attend" educational workshop or seminar. Offer to present this workshop free of charge as a value add for your partners and let them invite their community.

This approach is even better if you can bring two partners into the act. In this scenario, you can pitch a speech or seminar to each of them as a way to offer value to their clients and get some exposure to each partner's clients as well.

Curated Partnering

Building on the last two points, consider the impact of putting together an entire day of killer content. What if you went to your strategic partners and selected experts on a variety of subjects, then brought them together for a conference or other event? This curated conference could draw lots of attention from people interested in getting an entire day of useful information in one place.

Select or curate a big topic and bring in partners who are willing to introduce their networks to the daylong event. You can pack the house with what amounts to a group referral of all of the partners.

This method works equally well as a curated ebook of partner content that the entire partner group can share.

Incentivized Content

Some of the best content is that which your customers are willing to create and share. Something as simple and silly as a photo of customers using your products, or a contest rewarding the person who gets the most votes for a video featuring your services, is an effective way to create buzz while getting great referrals in the process.

The key is to structure the ask in a way that prompts referrals. For example, "Tell us the best use of our product. Show us your results. Tell us why you really want to win." This approach can generate some very powerful endorsements as people vie for a prize of some sort.

Content Inspiration

As soon as you start to embrace this idea of consistently finding and publishing educational content, I'm sure you'll start thinking about where to get ongoing inspiration for what to write about or collect.

The content themes we worked on earlier in this chapter will inform the kind of content you'll be on the lookout for, but it's also helpful to have a few go-to resources that can get the creative juices flowing when you run out of ideas.

Keep the following in mind as part of your inspiration routine.

1. RSS Reader: Remember tools like Feedly and Feedbin that we talked about earlier? Make an effort to use these as you scout out and subscribe to blogs related to your themes. Build folders in these tools in order to sort and sift by topic.
2. Curation Tools: A tool like Scoop.it allows you to find collections of content related to a variety of topics that others have put together.
3. Magazines: Don't forget about print magazines. Because digital gets all the play these days, print magazines have to work harder than ever to uncover unusual angles on topics that they have probably covered before. Subscribe to as many industry or customer-related journals as you can and find time to scan these.
4. Newsletters: Subscribe to industry and client newsletters and seek out some good newsletters that uncover other people's content, such as the series from SmartBrief.

5. Blog Aggregators: Sites like AllTop group the best blogs by subject and industry, making it very easy to scan entire collections of blog posts from one page.

6. Bookmarking Sites: Sites like Delicious, Reddit, and Diigo allow users to bookmark their favorite content from every corner of the Web and group it by topic or "tags." The popular or trending content rises to the top and effectively surfaces some great content with very little hunting on your part.

7. Sent E-mail Box: Finally, don't forget about your sent e-mail box. Quite often you've answered questions for your prospects and clients, sometimes months ago, that would make a great topic for a blog post. If your company has service support and technical people who handle these kinds of requests, buy them some pizza and get them to share the best or most frequently posed questions with you.

To get you started on understanding how teaching spreads in sales, here are my personal favorites for content similar to what's shared in this book.

- Duct Tape Selling—www.ducttapeselling.com (There's a blog just for this book, with lots of other resources as well.)
- EnMast—www.enmast.com
- The Sales Blog—thesalesblog.com
- The Bridge Group—blog.bridgegroupinc.com
- The Sales Archaeologist—www.omghub.com/sales-archaeologist -blog
- Smart Selling Tools—www.smartsellingtools.com/blog
- Co-Grow—www.collaborativegrowthnetwork.com
- Hubspot Blog—blog.hubspot.com/sales
- Caskey Sales Training—www.caskeyone.com
- Fresh Sales Strategies—www.jillkonrath.com/sales-blog
- Shift Selling Inc.—shiftselling.com
- Top Sales World—topsalesworld.com
- Score More Sales—scoremoresales.com
- B2B Lead Roundtable—b2bleadblog.com
- Selling Inbound—www.sellinbound.com
- RainToday—www.raintoday.com

Building Your Content Toolbox

I'll end this chapter on educational content with a rundown of some of the most helpful tools every content superstar should be familiar with.

Blogging

No surprise here . . . I'm going to ask you to create your own blog and use this as the foundational element of your content effort. There are a number of options, but I would find it hard to recommend any tool but Word-Press. WordPress's blogging platform is the leader in their field and comes complete with a community of developers creating and extending its usefulness beyond the core offering found at WordPress.org.

Images

Images attract attention. Every social network is testament to the fact that images draw more engagement than any other form of content. Gather as many photos of clients using your products or engaged during a teaching event as possible and start sharing these in your networking efforts. You can edit images using any number of desktop applications (such as Photoshop) but online options such as PicMonkey are much easier and cheaper to use.

You can find great images to use in blog posts and Facebook updates at PhotoPin.com or through paid services such as iStockphoto. You may also want to check out sites like Flickr or Google's Panoramio.com for storing images.

Infographics

If pictures tell a story, imagine a story told by data visualized as a picture. Infographics have become a very popular way to take data and turn it into something more attractive and, in some cases, more useful. Capture industry trends, product features, and comparison data and turn them into visually appealing stories for presentations and as content to help illustrate a point. Tools like Visual.ly and Piktochart make it very easy to create some of your own infographics.

Screencast

When you need to demonstrate how to do something on a computer, sometimes the best way is to present it visually. Capturing your screen, or screencasting, is a great way to create demo content. Tools such as Screen-Flow (on a Mac) and Camtasia (on a PC) are the go-to resources for this. Create a series of how-to screencasts that demonstrates product features or teaches key behind-the-scenes tips and training; these displays can go a long way toward demonstrating your expertise and provide more personalized help for your clients.

Online Seminars

The technology for holding meetings, presentations, and seminars online has come a long way. Today anyone can quickly and effectively produce highly educational content and attract an audience from anywhere in the world. The fact that tools like GoToWebinar and MeetingBurner also allow you to record and archive these sessions is a real bonus. Google+ Hangouts also gives you the ability to broadcast your sessions live to YouTube.

Audio Interviews

Capturing client and expert interviews is a great way to create easily portable content. Now that just about every prospect carries a smartphone, audio content is a very attractive option. Using a tool like Skype with the add-on Call Recorder (for Mac) or Pamela (PC version) you can conduct interviews over the phone and capture the entire session with ease.

Custom Surveys

Surveys are a great way to both learn what kind of content people are hungry for and to compile actual content from customers and prospects. Using a tool like Wufoo to create and employ forms or SurveyMonkey to collect survey data, you easily learn from customers and share insights from the market that journalists and prospects will eat up.

Transcription

Finally, don't forget to think about ways to repurpose things like audio and video interviews. Using a tool like Rev, you can order up text-based transcription of any audio or video file. Many times, an online seminar or audio interview can be tweaked a bit to create a great ebook or blog post.

PART II

PRACTICES OF THE NEW SALES GUIDE

Why Practicing Marketing
Is the New Way to Sales Success

I n the first section I covered the mind-sets of selling. What I described more than anything else are the shifts in thinking and strategic approach to sales that exist today.

In part II, we turn to the practices (some not always associated with traditional sales jobs) required for salespeople to excel in the new sales environment.

If part I was the strategy, part II is the tactics. These are the skills that sales guides need to acquire and practice daily to support and train in their sales teams.

Part II breaks down into the following five categories of tactical work.

Create a platform—It's no longer enough to be a part of the brand; today's salesperson needs to take charge of his or her own platform. This means creating an online presence that includes content, SEO, e-mail marketing, social media, and maybe even awareness advertising. These are the building blocks for creating an online reputation and community that moves beyond simply completing network profiles.

Become an authority—One of the most important ways to shift the context of the sales job is to build your expertise and reputation for sharing useful information. This is how you start the process of being invited to share your ideas before your competition knows there is an opportunity to do so. You become an authority by authoring educational articles, speaking at industry and community events, and even facilitating things like Google+ Hangout discussions among customers and prospects.

Mine networks—The new suite of online tools makes it much easier to listen to entire markets, to drill down and discover invaluable intelligence about what people need, whom they report to, and what their objectives for the year are. Salespeople must get very good at listening for clues and mining networks to create interdepartmental relationships and to connect the dots between those who need help and those whom they can help.

Build your Sales Hourglass—Prospects have gotten very good at figuring out solutions to the problems they've identified, due in large part to unprecedented amounts of data and information available online. Today's sales professional has to understand and build cases for problems that the market doesn't yet know exist and then guide prospects on a journey that leads to the creation of loyal, repeat customers. This is a skill that comes from helping customers think bigger about what's possible.

Finish the sale—I've always contended that a sale is not a sale until the customer receives a result. This means that you have to get involved in the experience before, during, and after the commitment or sale is made. Staying connected in this manner is also how you get more referrals and better understand the future needs of a client.

There's no question that what I'm describing is going to require a new view of the role of a sales professional, many aspects of which we covered in part I. It's impossible to implement these practices without also accepting that organizations need to hire differently, train differently, and measure success differently in order to change the context of selling both internally and externally.

CHAPTER 8

Create an Expert Platform

n November 2007, Andrew McKay arrived in Wasaga Beach, Ontario, Canada, from the UK with a business network that consisted of his wife and young child.

Although he had never worked in real estate before, he decided he wanted to get into the field. He received his real estate license in June 2008. Initially he was taught by others in the industry through the traditional methods of networking: local clubs, parent groups, and the like. He realized, after some consideration, that every real estate agent in the area was using the same outreach strategy. He had to find a way to differentiate himself.

McKay found a Web service called Real Estate Tomato that taught him about blogging. He started blogging about real estate and also about what was happening in his community. He quickly became known as a local real estate expert and started to get inquiries from out-of-area buyers. It seems that when these buyers went online to research agents in the area, his sizable presence and platform drew them in. After all, people searching online had no loyalty to any long-established local agents, so Andrew's online presence and content made him valuable to buyers before they even met him.

In 2011, he was named the top salesperson in his Century 21 office in just his third year in the business. The two runners-up for the award had a combined fifty years in the business.

As you've probably surmised by now, it's no longer enough to be part of a brand. Today's salesperson needs to take charge of his or her own platform. This means creating an online presence that includes content, SEO, e-mail marketing, social media, and maybe even awareness advertising. These are the building blocks for creating an online reputation and community that moves beyond simply completing network profiles.

Many salespeople have been taught that content creation pretty much begins and ends with lots of updates on LinkedIn. While this is a logical place for salespersons to hang out and engage with their community, this idea alone completely misses the opportunity described throughout this book.

The complete platform approach that I outline in this chapter goes against the grain of what most salespeople have been led to believe is their arena. In fact, the plan outlined in this chapter has a lot in common with a plan I would outline for experts in any field who are trying to build a name for themselves—and that's precisely the point.

Before you start down the path of creating a content platform, you must consider why you're doing it. It's not just about creating content, but rather doing so smartly, with the purpose of putting a big footprint in the space you're active in. Your goal is to establish a name that appears frequently alongside trusted material.

If you want to rise above the level of the typical sales professional and become an asset both to your clients and your company, you must embrace this "expert in the works" mind-set.

What follows is a step-by-step guide for how to create your very own expert platform.

Your Basic Platform Setup

Blogging

Every marketing department and every sales manager should be teaching, encouraging, and facilitating active blogging from every member of the sales team.

In a perfect world, someone in the marketing department would come to you and say, "Hey, we need you to start blogging, and here's how." This tactic is certainly best employed with full support and orchestration from marketing, but lacking that, the smart sales professional needs to figure out how to get into the game on her own.

A blog is the best starting place for online content these days and content, as we know, is the name of the game when it comes to inbound selling. Don't worry that at first you won't have a large and eager readership. While that's often seen as a reason to blog, it doesn't really matter for you at the very start. Initially, your blog may have very few readers, or even no readers at all. But fear not: the act of blogging is about producing assets, not about "being a blogger." Take that mind-set into your work and you won't worry so much about why you're putting in the time.

Creating a consistent blogging habit is how you get found by search engines, have something worth sharing in social media, and begin to build a body of work to draw from in many ways.

WHAT'S IT ABOUT?

The first thing you need to decide on is an overall theme for your blog. Obviously, it should relate to your industry and what you sell, but that's just the starting point. If you sell truck parts, for example, you probably don't want to write the world's greatest truck-parts blog. However, you may find that no one else seems to be writing about trends in technical innovation in four-wheel-drive trucks. Think outside your actual product or service—think about the clarity of your offering.

You'll want to think in terms of a narrower focus, something that can encompass a narrow but important content theme. If you want blogging to pay off over the long haul (and that's why we're doing this), you have to resist the urge to view your blog as a place to journal and perhaps to veer off the topic—a tendency you'll see on many blogs.

Blogging is a sales tool, pure and simple. This is how people are going to start to differentiate you from the pack. Treat it as such.

GET THE TECH PART DONE

The second order of business, after nailing down the primary focus of your blog, is to set it up so you can start using it.

Owning your own domain name (perhaps your full name.com) and the content you produce is the ultimate option when it comes to your own reputation and platform building. I urge you to consider this option first.

As I mentioned in the previous chapter, my blogging tool of choice is the self-hosted WordPress. You can find it for free at WordPress.org. Other options include the hosted version at WordPress.com and micro-blog tools like Tumblr.

A self-hosted WordPress.org site gives you the most flexibility and control. You simply get Web hosting, install the software, and blog away on any domain that you personally own. Many hosting companies, such as HostGator and Bluehost, have a one-button WordPress install so the technical aspect isn't really that high a hurdle.

The trade-off is that using a self-hosted site means there is a little more to do, from a technical standpoint, than with a hosted site. The good news is that there is plenty of information available that will walk even the most tech-nervous creature on the planet through the process. I suggest you start by visiting WordPress's wpbeginner.com.

BUT I'M NOT A WRITER

Now that you have a blogging platform set, it's time to get down to the writing.

I can hear the gears in your head turning, but here's the deal. It doesn't matter if you think you're not a writer. You're not writing the next great novel. You're writing explanations to topics you see coming up in your field all the time. You're taking questions that prospects ask and providing answers in plain English that anyone can understand. (We'll cover more on how to be a more productive writer, and the benefits of writing, later in this section.)

Sure, you need your writing to be clear, easy to understand, and free of obvious grammar disasters, but you don't have to be a great writer. If you've been able to effectively explain and simplify complex solutions in your sales approach, then just write like you speak.

Start off with 300- to 500-word posts unless your topic is highly technical and needs a longer explanation. As you get in the habit of posting to your blog, you'll find sitting down to write posts gets easier. You'll also see that the occasional 1,000-word (or greater) post actually gets the most traffic.

The easiest way to structure your shorter blog posts is to organize them around a benefit-laden headline such as *7 RIDICULOUSLY PRACTICAL WAYS TO USE SOCIAL MEDIA IN YOUR SALES JOB.*

From there, you only need an opening that sums up why this post is important, seven points that make up the outline of the post, and then a conclusion that restates why the topic is important. It's not much more complicated than that. Start with your main point, add four or five subheadings that act as the outline, and fill in the blanks.

At first, aim for at least three blog posts a week. You're not a news media site, so you don't need more than that, but you do need to think about building up your total volume. Three posts a week over the period of a year will give you the pages needed to compete in searches.

NOW FOR SOME EXTENSIONS

One of the reasons so many people use WordPress to run their entire site is that the platform is structured in such a way that anyone with some coding skills can create plug-ins that extend the functionality of the core WordPress platform.

Initially this won't be very important, but there are three plug-ins I recommend for every business blog. Adding plug-ins is very simple, and sites like wpbeginner.com, as well as the plug-in creators, offer advice on how to add and configure plug-ins.

The three I recommend are: WordPress SEO by Yoast, WordPress's Contextually Related Posts, and Sociable.

1. WordPress SEO by Yoast gives you to the ability to make each and every post a little more optimized for the keywords you want to show up in searches.
2. Contextually Related Posts takes your current post and automatically adds five posts that are related. Obviously, this gets better as you add more posts, but this can really help people go deeper into your content.
3. Sociable allows you to add sharing buttons for most of the major social and content networks so that people can easily tweet, "like," and +1 your content to their networks.

THEME OF A DIFFERENT KIND

So far we've been talking a lot about themes in terms of content, but WordPress uses the term "theme" to describe the template for the look and feel of the blog.

Once you have the blog installed, you'll want to own the look and feel. You can hire a WordPress designer to create or customize your site, but chances are you can also find a nice fit at a premium-theme site such as StudioPress or WooThemes.

When it comes to themes, the most important thing to consider is how the look and "feel" matches your industry. If you sell professional services, you want a theme that clearly means business. If, however, you sell a high-tech product that resonates with a certain audience, you want a theme that matches that feel. Most of the professional-theme sites categorize themes to match industries.

After you purchase a theme from a theme designer, you upload the files to your domain and in most cases edit for things like color, font, and header graphics. Every theme is a little different, but theme sites like StudioPress generally provide instruction on how to customize your templates.

REVIST YOUR CONTENT THEMES

Okay, now that we've covered the look-and-feel theme, let's go back to your content themes. If you took my advice to heart and created your twelve foundational content themes, as discussed in chapter seven, then you already have a broad editorial calendar for the next year.

That's right: in a way, your entire year of blogging is already mapped out. That's not to say that you'll take it month by month in the beginning. After all, you need to get round one of your content created before you can slip into an annual plan.

Creating this editorial calendar means you have ideas for your first twelve posts as a way to get started. You should revisit your monthly themes at the start of each month, but I find that initially you'll want to write one good post for each theme to lay the foundation for your entire year of blogging. Each post should cover something specifically related to your twelve themes so that you have something to lean on as you come back later to revisit each theme.

TELL THE WORLD

Once you've created a handful of posts, you need to start letting people know about your blog. Ask close associates, customers, and strategic partners to visit your site and give you feedback on the overall usefulness of the content as well as the look and feel of the site.

You're not looking for compliments here: be open to the good, the bad, and the ugly. It's the only way you'll get better and the only way you'll know if you're on the right track in the first place.

We're going to cover social networks later in this chapter, but once your blog has a look and content that your close allies and clients approve of, spread the word widely to Twitter, LinkedIn, Facebook, and Google+ each time you have new content to share. If you've been sharing other people's content, as I suggested in chapter six, sharing a new blog post will just be part of the routine.

Podcasting—It's Just an Audio Blog Post!

The next piece of your foundational content platform is a podcast. Now, don't get hung up on the term; it's not as technical or time-consuming as you think.

Think a podcast won't help you sell?

Bill Caskey, president of Caskey Sales Training, had been doing his Advanced Selling podcast for a few months back in 2010. Although his listener numbers were going up, he wasn't getting many calls from listeners about purchasing training, which was one of his primary goals.

He decided to do a podcast "just for sales managers" and asked listeners to forward that episode to their managers. Within two weeks, three sales managers had called him and he had booked two consulting gigs: a year-long engagement for $75,000, and a sales rollout meeting for about $10,000. All from one episode.

It was the calls that caused him to say, "We're on to something here." Podcasting is unique because by the time someone calls you to find out more about what you do, he feels as if he knows you. And that's the best positioning you can have.

I've been publishing the Duct Tape Marketing podcast since 2005. I got into podcasting as a way to create content and unlock opportunities to get in front of leading authors and industry experts.

Back then, podcasting was new, iTunes had just burst onto the scene, and an army of podcasters embraced it as a way to syndicate content. When social media came along, though, platforms like Twitter and Facebook made podcasting seem so last decade.

But a funny thing happened on the way to the evolution of all things digital. People started to rediscover podcasting as a tremendous way to package and deliver content in a new and intimate way. All of a sudden, everyone had a podcast listening device (otherwise known as a smartphone) in their pocket, and the new iPhone even came with the iTunes Podcast app preloaded. With the easy access, podcast listenership again began to surge.

Some people shy away from the term "podcast" in the same way they avoided "blog." Here's the deal: as with a blog, it doesn't matter what you call a podcast. Creating audio content is a great way to tap into the fact that people want to listen to content on their most personal device—their phone. Why wouldn't you work your tail off to get invited into that space?

Podcasting is simply creating audio content—portable to any smartphone—that is easy to share and even easier to listen to. In fact, for many people it's the preferred form of content consumption. Some people just don't have the time or inclination to read, but they do listen to audio content when they use the treadmill, commute to and from work, or walk the dog.

THE SECRET ABOUT PODCASTING

One of the things that nobody tells you about podcasting is that it's an ultraeffective way to get in front of people you want to meet. Think about that pioneer in your community, maybe even in your company. If you sent her an e-mail and said something like, "Hey, can you spare fifteen minutes so I can ask you a few questions?" how far do you think that would go?

But what if you sent her an e-mail that said "Can I interview you for my podcast?" It's an entirely different request, with the same net effect for you. People are much more eager to be interviewed for content that will be viewed and used by others (and that they can share with their own networks). If you ask in this manner, you're more likely to get to sit down with someone who can help you raise your status and your exposure—and perhaps even boost your effectiveness as a salesperson.

Over the years, I've interviewed many authors for my podcast because I wanted to be an author myself. The people who helped me get there faster than I would have on my own were authors I interviewed before anyone had heard of me. People like Tom Peters, Guy Kawasaki, and Seth Godin granted me interviews because I promised to promote what they were working on at the time. Asking them for brief interviews opened the doors to long-term relationships.

You don't have to try to land well-known authors or anyone famous, just focus on doing interviews with people whose work matters to your own goals. Think about industry analysts, the influencers that your customers pay attention to, or CEOs of companies you would like to target. Sending interview requests to people like that can be key in building your reputation as well as increasing the overall value of your content platform.

HOW TO CREATE A PODCAST

There are dozens of ways to podcast. While I can't possibly share every aspect of the technology, I can outline how I create my podcast, and describe the tools I use, so that you can get started quickly.

Each podcast episode is about twenty minutes in length, as I find that's how long people can stay tuned in. Podcasts are fairly easily to produce with inexpensive equipment and easy-to-use software:

Blue Yetti USB Microphone—This a high-quality microphone with lots of professional settings; it will set you back about a hundred dollars, but the quality sound is worth it.

Skype—Because my guests come from all over the world, I do all of my interviews over Skype. I use a SkypeIn nine-digit phone number so my guests can call from a phone, if they wish (they can also connect directly via Skype). I also use a Skype add-on called Call Recorder so that I can record directly in Skype and then split the tracks to edit them independently (the PC version of this tool is called Pamela).

Garage Band—I edit on a Mac, and the Garage Band editing program provides everything I need. I level the sound, add music, and edit out unwanted sound before saving to iTunes. There's a similar free tool for PCs called Audacity.

Libsyn—I use this service to host and stream my podcast. I pay about $10 a month, and it keeps my podcast separate from my Web hosting.

Blubrry PowerPress—This WordPress plug-in creates a player for my blog and handles the RSS technical stuff, including posting the podcast to iTunes. I run my podcast on my regular blog and use the category RSS feed to splice those posts off.

Rev.com—Sometimes I transcribe my podcasts, repurposing one form of content to another. Rev.com is fast and very affordable.

If you want to learn more about the technical aspects of podcasting, check out the **Podcast Answer Man,** Cliff Ravenscraft.

I publish my podcast episodes to my WordPress blog, and I recommend this approach. The podcast, which I generally publish on Wednesdays, looks like one of my regular blog posts, but with an audio player embedded so that people can listen to or download the MP3 file that is the audio portion of the show.

SPREADING THE WORD

The thing that really powers podcasts is the fact that once people subscribe to your podcast feed, they receive each new episode automatically. It's absolutely essential that you get your podcast RSS feed listed in iTunes, through which about 90 percent of all shows are heard. As of this writing, Apple reported topping one billion podcast subscriptions via its iTunes store.

If you are running your podcast on WordPress, as I've suggested, there's a bonus: you can easily create a podcast category that will act as the RSS feed for your podcast separate from the RSS feed for your blog. For instance, my blog feed is ducttapemarketing.com/blog/feed and my podcast feed is ducttapemarketing.com/blog/category/podcast.

My Personal Listening List

Just as subscribing to and reading blogs will make you a better blogger, subscribing to and listening to podcasts will make you a better podcaster.

The following podcasts have become very popular in iTunes and offer tremendous content for those inclined to consume content while driving, working out, or simply hanging out, plugged into a pair of earbuds.

Seth Godin's Startup School: The Startup School podcast features highlights from a workshop Godin conducted with thirty up-and-coming entrepreneurs.

The Social Media Marketing Podcast by Michael Stelzner: *Social Media Examiner*'s Michael Stelzner helps your business navigate the social jungle with success stories and expert interviews with leading social media pros.

The Human Business Way by Chris Brogan: Business with a soul. Improve your impact. Be brave. Tell bigger stories. Discussions and more with today's top authorities on sales, marketing, and much more than just business.

The Advanced Selling Podcast: This is a must-subscribe for B2B salespeople. Every week, Bill Caskey and Bryan Neale take on a wide variety of sales topics.

This Is Your Life by Michael Hyatt: A weekly podcast dedicated to intentional leadership. The goal is to help you live with more passion, work with greater focus, and lead with extraordinary influence.

Pat Flynn's Smart Passive Income: Flynn reveals all of his online business and blogging strategies, income sources, and killer marketing tips and tricks so you can stay ahead of the curve with your online business or blog.

Duct Tape Marketing: And of course, I'm partial to my own podcast full of small-business marketing tips, tactics, resources, and interviews with some of today's most inspiring authors, leaders, and thinkers.

Download the iTunes podcast app or Stitcher app and start filling your head with the sounds of content in the form of podcasts.

Thoughts on List Building

I know the thought of building your own e-mail list of noncustomers might seem like new territory, but it's key to building expertise. The more people you know, the more chances there are that someone on your list, reading your great content, is going to know the perfect buyer for your products and services. By expanding the traditional reach of the salesperson to include a universe of people interested in the topics you can teach, you increase your chances of expanding your lead and customer base. At the end of the day, the more people on your personal e-mail list, the more influence you wield.

Getting more e-mail subscribers is job number one.

Acquiring the contact information of someone who has expressed at least a mild interest in what you do and has given you permission to tell him a great deal more about what you do is the first and perhaps most important task. Traditionally, e-mail leads would come to you through a marketing effort, but I'm talking about expanding that notion greatly.

There are few salespeople today who can get by on marketing-generated leads alone. Today's salesperson must get access, permission, and time on the screen and must have multiple opportunities to build enough relationship capital to convert trust into a sale.

E-mail marketing, combined, of course, with advertising, referrals, public relations, and a total online presence is the complete package.

List building is an essential element of e-mail marketing today and takes a strategic approach that's in line with its importance.

GIVE ME A REASON TO SUBSCRIBE

It's no longer enough to slap an e-mail sign-up form on every page of your website and call it done. You must focus attention on detail and expand your thinking on list building to get your "value exchange" or "reason I would give up my e-mail address" in front of more of the right people at just the right time.

ADDRESS PRIVACY ISSUES

Everyone is leery about privacy and spam. You know you don't intend to spam your subscribers or sell their e-mail addresses to others. Tell them so right on your form.

SHOW SAMPLES

Once you've created and sent a few newsletters, use your e-mail service provider's archive functionality to create online versions of your newsletter and invite people to click on a link that shows them the content they can expect to get from you when they subscribe.

More Thoughts on List Building

Now that you've got the basics of list building down, think about adding one or more of these advanced list-building techniques.

FEATURE WITH CONTENT

By this point, you should have started producing high-quality, educational content, the kind that draws links and readers. Now, as people engage with your content, you'll want to explore ways to promote your list sign-up.

Many WordPress theme frameworks, such as Genesis and Thesis, allow for "feature boxes." These boxes make it easy to place a sign-up box at, say, the end of each blog post or at the top of your blog home page. Placing your e-mail offer where people read and enjoy your content improves subscription.

CONTENT PARTNER SHARE

One of the most important ways to entice e-mail subscribers today is by offering long-format content in the shape of an ebook. Generally, this is content that tackles one subject deeply and in a way that's appealing to your target client.

Once you've gone to the effort to produce this content, reach out to other businesses, the ones that know they should be offering content to their customers, and allow them to promote your ebook by way of a special cobranded sign-up landing page.

RECOMMEND PARTNERS

Once someone signs up to receive your offer, it's good form to redirect her to a thank-you page that gives her assurance that all is well, tells her what to expect next, or other details.

Consider partnering with three or four other high-quality content producers that you would recommend to your readers and suggest subscriptions to these partners on your thank-you page. For example, RainToday and Jill Konrath are both excellent resources when it comes to learning more about sales.

If each of the partners involved performs this action, you'll see more subscribers by way of referral.

ADVERTISE

Once you've established that people value the content you are producing (meaning they tell you so, stay subscribed, and even share your content with others), you may find that advertising is an effective way to create list sign-ups. This assumes that your conversion and measurement activities are such that you have at least some idea of what an e-mail subscriber is worth, in the long run, to your selling effort.

You can effectively promote an ebook or other content through Facebook Promoted Posts or by purchasing solo ads in newsletters related to your market.

ENDORSEMENT SWAPS

One of the most powerful ways to quickly add subscribers is for another list owner—someone who's built trust with his or her own subscribers—to send a mailing endorsing your ebook or newsletter content.

Now, while this is obviously a great tactic, it's one that requires consideration. No list owner will risk his or her reputation by endorsing low-quality content, and neither should you. This is a tactic that takes time, as it's best done with partners with whom you've established a trusting relationship, either by way of reputation in your industry or by your directly working together on other projects.

Approach your partners with the idea of sending an e-mail offering their great content to your list, while they do the same for you.

Landing Pages

Another element that's become a staple in the inbound-content game is the landing page. The concept is pretty straightforward: a landing page is a page that you want people to visit to take some specific act. For example, landing pages are often used to offer a free video course, ebook, or even a newsletter subscription.

My recommendation is that you add a landing page to create newsletter sign-ups and then promote that page in social media and to your existing network or circle of influence.

As you build your content library with materials such as white papers and ebooks, educational courses, or online seminars, you can start using landing pages for each of these elements as well.

Any page you create for a website can be a landing page, including a specific blog post, and there are services, such as Unbounce and Lead-Pages, that can help you automate, design, test, and track your landing page campaigns and conversions. These specialized services may well be worth the cost when it comes to creating the most effective landing pages.

There's a bit of art and science to what makes a landing page work, so testing and tweaking will always be required, but the following tips should help you get started optimizing your landing pages.

Landing Page Optimization

Only one thing—Your landing page should do one thing and one thing only: get a subscriber, offer an ebook, or create an enrollment for an event. Use every bit of its real estate to sell that call to action. Don't try to introduce other options or you will find your pages will confuse your visitors.

Test variations—You must test multiple variations of your page elements at all times. One of the easiest ways to do this is by using a tool that offers simple A/B testing. The services mentioned above make this process very simple.

Message and ad—It may be a good idea to have individual landing pages for each ad you are running. When the landing page copy specifically matches the ad copy that brought viewers there, conversions will very likely follow. And tweaking your ads is just another part of the testing.

Use video—It's been proven in many studies that video on landing pages increases conversion. This is due to the fact that your call to action can be explained, you build trust when the visitor sees and hears a real person, and video is simply more engaging and harder to ignore than text. (Make sure you test your videos too!)

Make it easy—Make sure that what you want the visitor to do is obvious—and how to do it should be even more obvious. This is where the use of video, audio, arrows, and buttons can be effective. Limit any data collection to name and e-mail or your conversions will drop; that is, unless what you are offering is so valuable people will readily give more information.

Offer sharing—You'll want to make it easy for a visitor to tweet, share, and forward your page and their actions on your page. Add as much social networking functionality as possible. This is where the landing page services can come in handy.

Pay them back—After your visitor takes the prescribed action, you should direct him or her to a conversion or thank-you page. But don't waste that space—use it to create even more engagement by offering an unexpected freebie ebook or download of some sort.

For more information, here are three useful books on this topic: *Landing Page Optimization* by Tim Ash, *Always Be Testing* by Bryan Eisenberg, and *Web Analytics 2.0* by Avinash Kaushik.

Content Networks

Now that you're a full-fledged inbound content producer, let's expand the view of content to include content networks. Content networks are popular sites where anyone with an account can publish, share, curate, and, most important, embed content produced by you or by others.

Embedding content simply means that the content producer gives you permission to take a little bit of code and paste it into your website to embed a video, list, or presentation deck in a blog post or on any page. Ease of sharing is what makes this so attractive.

To take advantage of this opportunity, start by creating accounts for each of the following content networks. As you did with your profile on social networks, take a few minutes to personalize and enhance your profile on each network. Remember, this will immediately give you a handful of new outposts for sharing your content and for finding and transporting other people's useful content. It's definitely worth your time.

YouTube: I'm guessing you've watched a YouTube video at some point in your life, but you may not have set up your own channel. Create a branded channel for your content efforts and then start uploading any relevant video content you've created. Also, find and "like" content your marketing department has created.

You can also look up content created by your customers and competitors, as well as other industry-related videos. These might make sense for your blogging efforts or as content to highlight in your newsletter or on your Facebook page.

SlideShare: SlideShare is the network of choice for PowerPoint presentations. It can make great sense for you to upload decks from sales and product demonstrations, online seminars, or other educational workshops you've created.

You can embed your presentations in your blog posts and find and embed other people's presentations as well.

Listly: Listly is a service that makes it easy for people to compile and share lists of websites or tools or even just tips. People really seem to like lists, so it's great to get in the habit of compiling a few lists and finding great lists that have already been compiled and curated by others.

Visual.ly: Visual.ly is your option for finding infographics—images created using data. Infographics are very popular. You can create basic infographics from research findings that your organization produced or by searching for relevant visualizations on the site. These images are easily embedded. The site also allows you to find designers you can work with to design your own infographics.

Embed.ly : Finally, do you need to embed a video, PDF, audio, or even article abstract into a blog post? There's an app for that! With Embed, the hard work is done for you. All you do is find the content; the tool creates a professional-looking embed. There's even a WordPress plug-in.

Social Networks

We will get deep into social networks in upcoming chapters, but first I want to address the creation of a social profile or bio on the most popular social networks as part of your content platform. (For full coverage on how to build an effective profile, jump back to chapter five.)

Facebook—If your company has a Facebook page, and something tells me they probably do, you may want to consider creating your own. If you use a personal Facebook page, then now is not the time to try to mix the two.

LinkedIn—Chances are you already have a somewhat active LinkedIn profile. It's the one social network that's always been about professional networking—something every salesperson knows he or she needs to do.

Google+—While Google+ lags behind other networks in terms of buzz and engagement, it is still growing rapidly and it is still owned by Google. There is substantial evidence to suggest that Google is attaching search bonus points to content shared and +1'd on its home turf.

Twitter—Twitter is a great platform for establishing your sharing routine. Make it a point to share your content on Twitter, but also to share ten or twelve pieces from other people—particularly other people you might consider strategic partners or who are friends in the industry.

Until you build any kind of following of your own, think of Twitter as a networking tool that can put you on the radar of people you might want as guest bloggers or podcast guests.

Because you've built a list of blogs that are fed to your RSS reader, you can use a tool like Buffer to preschedule tweets so that you can publish throughout the day, even though you scan your reader (Feedly or Feedbin) before breakfast each day.

Vertical—Almost every industry has a social network of some sort. Do some research to find appropriate niche networks put together by industry players, associations, or trade shows and consider joining these if your customers and prospects are found there.

Amplifying Your Content

It's worth noting that, once you create content, you need to have a routine to promote and amplify it.

Below is a sampling of my content amplification routine. I follow these steps for each new blog post I write in an effort to get that particular piece of content the greatest amount of exposure. Is this the perfect, all-inclusive practice? Probably not, but it's a routine that can be completed in about five minutes. Plus, it gives my content a chance to be seen by many potential clients, journalists, and strategic partners.

After I hit "publish" on a new piece of content, I tweet the headline of my post with a link, always adding a few words of context to further clarify why someone might be interested in my post, in HootSuite.

A sample tweet: [Headline] How to Anchor Your Brand with a Great Story—[context] one that lets people join something as a way of expressing values—[URL] www.ducttapemarketing.com/blog . . .

I then

- Publish the post to my Facebook page
- Publish the post to my Google+ stream: public, circles, and extended circles
- Publish the post to my LinkedIn profile and also share it with several large groups
- Bookmark the post in appropriate tags to Delicious or Reddit

If a post has drawn a large number of retweets, I may post it to Twitter a second time during the day. If I do, I usually schedule the tweet for a specific time, using HootSuite's scheduling function.

Some points worth noting about my amplification strategy in general:

1. I don't use a service or tool to cross-post the content to all avenues. I think the social networks have their own personality and followings, so it's key to take a minute to point out something different about the post in each network (although HootSuite could do this for me).
2. I participate in many other ways, unrelated to my own content promotion, in each of these networks. For example, I often comment on other people's content, make observations, ask questions, and share posts I think are useful.
3. I check on the post (or podcast) several times a day, depending on my schedule, to participate in any conversations happening around the content, including comments on the original blog post.
4. I include Twitter, Google+, LinkedIn, and Facebook buttons under every blog post.
5. I have links to share the content with popular bookmarking sites on the blog posts (Sociable plug-in) and in the RSS feed (Feedburner FeedFlare option).
6. I often highlight a particularly well-read blog post or two from the week in my weekly e-mail newsletter.

Outsource Content

Surely by now someone reading this book is wondering whether he or she couldn't simply hire someone to do all this content creation.

The simple answer is yes, but with a caution.

What I mean by that is that you're the only one who knows the list of themes, questions, pain points, and insight needed to make this worth taking the time to do in the first place. You can delegate certain elements to others, but you can never abdicate inbound content creation to a hired gun.

If you decide to get some help from outside services or individuals, here's how I recommend you proceed.

- Create a list of proposed titles for blog posts or articles and briefly describe the context of the articles.
- Using a service like Zerys, InboundWriter, or Blog Mutt, identify a few potential writers to audition as your writer.
- When you receive your articles, don't just cut and paste them to your blog automatically. Take the time to go over each piece and edit for specifics, tone of voice, and your personal touch.
- If you find a particular writer who seems to work well for you, you may decide to set up a routine with that person, perhaps contracting with him for a certain number of blog posts per month.

Even if you go with an outside content creator, I still encourage you to create one very thorough post on your own each week. The research and the need to explain something in your own terms in writing (and in speaking) will benefit you in the long run. We'll see this as well in the next chapter.

Your Best Sales Tool

No matter how enamored you may be with social media, and as useful as blogging and podcasting are and will continue to be, e-mail still out-punches just about every tool out there when it comes to cost-effective lead conversion.

Done correctly, what this really requires is effectively using e-mail communication in conjunction with efforts to produce educational content, amplify content throughout social media channels, and turn Twitter followers into e-mail subscribers.

Effective integration makes e-mail work, but there are a handful of things you need to do to get the most out of the e-mail component of the mix.

Newsletters

The next kind of content needed for your foundation strategy is consistent e-mail communication. Most of the time this is accomplished through a newsletter that delivers a set amount of content at a set interval, using a fairly consistent format.

I recommend you start a newsletter right away and use it as a way to share your blog posts, other people's content, and news about customers. Plan on creating a monthly publication at the very least and working up to weekly publication once you get the hang of it. If you're blogging with any regularity, you can always add one of your blog posts, along with several other relevant posts you've discovered in your RSS reading, to fill out the content for the week.

GRAB ATTENTION

It's not enough to have an e-mail subscribe form tucked into the sidebar of your home page. If you've got a great offer to put in front of your visitors, you need to make it impossible to ignore, but without being obnoxious.

New pop-ups make grabbing visitor attention—and turning it into e-mail list subscribing—almost pleasant. For example, consider the WordPress plug-in called Pippity. Once installed and configured, this tool will note when you have a visitor who has not been offered your e-mail subscription and will briefly take over the screen to make her an offer. The visitor can close the pop-up window without taking any action, but this tool positions your list in a way that's hard to ignore.

I know there are some people who don't like this tactic, but Pippity gives you so much control, including A/B testing, that you can fine-tune the tool to make it work for you. Like it or not, with the right offer, most people see 300 percent to 400 percent jumps in subscribers when they use this kind of approach. (One tip: turn it off for mobile browsers. As of this writing, there appears to be no way to make it a pleasant experience on a mobile.)

EXCHANGE VALUE

Giving people a reason to subscribe is even more important than simply grabbing their attention. In order to get willing subscribers these days, you need to sell the value of what you have to offer and most likely exchange something—a free ebook or report—right at the point of subscription.

The act of giving out an e-mail address comes with a price these days because all of our e-mail in-boxes are jammed. Your free stuff better sound as good as most people's paid stuff if you want to get subscribers.

Of course, if you expect to keep subscribers, you need to keep the value exchange high. Turning e-mail subscribers into paying customers is not a one-time event; it's accomplished through a process of building trust over time.

No matter what time frame you choose to offer your e-mail newsletter—whether it's once a week or once a month—each issue should be something that people look forward to receiving. It's great to have a large list of subscribers, but if less than 10 percent actually open your e-mails, you won't get much return on your efforts. Make it worth their while.

BE SHARABLE

Smart marketers have always employed tools that made it easier for people to share their e-mail newsletter with friends. These days that means making your content easy to share in social media as well.

Most e-mail service providers have added sharing options that you can embed in your content so that a reader can tweet that he just read your article. Most service providers also allow you to create an online archive version of your newsletter that you can use to socialize your content sent via e-mail.

GO SOLO

Once your readers come to appreciate your valuable newsletter content, you may earn the right to send them offers. This is something that takes a little bit of experimentation and trust. You certainly risk eroding your good reputation by sending too many offers or by sending offers that just don't make sense.

While you can mix an offer or two into your regular e-mail newsletter format, I've found that sending the occasional offer for a product, program, or even joint venture with a product or service you truly believe in, using what is called a solo e-mail, is the best approach.

A solo e-mail is designed to do only one thing: deliver the story and make a case for your offer. This can be a straight-out offer to buy a product or even an announcement for a free online seminar where you intend to make an offer, but it must be about one thing and one thing only.

Let me repeat: sending offers is something you earn, just as you earned the subscriber in the first place. You must take care to treat this trust with respect or you will lose it. Keep the value of your offers as high as the value of your content and your readers will appreciate getting both.

As you can see, this platform building isn't for the faint of heart. There's a lot a work to do, but that's part of what makes it such a powerful tactic. How many of your competitors will take the time to do the things detailed in this chapter? My guess is very few and that's what will allow you to stand out and build the kind of expertise and authority that will change the very nature of the relationships you're able to build in the market.

CHAPTER 9

Become an Authority

When Kasey Bayne started blogging for her employer, FreshBooks, it was simply to build out a new sales and business development channel. However, as she continued to plug away at it, she discovered that it was slowly evolving into something bigger.

Suddenly she found that she was not only attending conferences, but speaking at them, guesting on podcasts, and winning awards—not just for the product (which won its own awards!) but for the work she was doing creating content.

She was named to the Top 40 Under 40 by CPA Practice Advisor and listed in *Accounting Today*'s Top 100 Ones to Watch. This industry recognition helped her land a highly sought-after position at small business-focused cloud- and iPad-centric accounting software developer Kashoo.

Bayne's authority even merited coverage in *Accounting Today*'s news service, where she had this to say about the move: "I had a great run at FreshBooks and I can't say enough good things about them, but I get to do some great things at Kashoo, where I'll be taking on more of a leadership role and really be a part of helping to build the company."

So you see, Bayne was able to build authority and a personal brand that not only made her more valuable to other firms, but moved with her to her new position.

That's the power of building authority in any industry, something every salesperson today can do.

One of the most important ways to shift the context of the sales job is to build an expertise and a reputation for sharing useful information. It's a fact of doing business that we give more credibility to the ideas of those we consider authorities.

A best-selling author gets paid a lot more to speak at an event than someone we've never heard of. It doesn't necessarily mean the published author's ideas are any better than the other person's; it's that we assign value to the fact that others think the author is an authority as well.

The salesperson who travels the path that leads to increasing her exposure and authority can benefit in the same way the best-selling author did. You may never have the ambition to write a book, but by authoring educational articles, speaking at industry and community events, and even by facilitating Google+ Hangout discussions among customers and prospects, you can increase your status as an expert. Participating in activities that help your customers get what they want is how you turn your authority into a competitive advantage.

Samantha Ashdown owns a residential real estate business in the UK called Home Truths (www.home-truths.co.uk). She creates authority by showing her competition how to do what she does—free of charge. In turn, she reaps the benefit of all the associated buzz. Samantha explains her strategy:

"I have something I call my 'Click-through Rate Challenge [CTR].' I send out with my Supertips a free 'how-to' guide to help agents improve their click-through rates on the portals. My experience tells me that a 5% CTR on a property means the agent is usually struggling to generate viewings on it, whereas a 10% often means a steady stream of viewings, and an offer in the not-too-distant future. My record CTR was 25%, which was the highest ever recorded on the main UK property portal (Rightmove) and my strategy is very simple and clear. I ask agents to challenge me to increase theirs—free of charge—which creates interest and buzz, and unfailingly the agent is thrilled by the results. I love it!"

Why You Must Write

I've spent a great deal of ink in this book on the subject of content creation. It's that important to your success.

The practice of writing daily may or may not turn you into what anyone calls a writer. But the habit of writing will shape more than your ability to create meaningful content. Writing to express your thoughts will transform everything about how you approach business and train you to view the world, and your place in it, in a completely different way. That's the reason I believe that every salesperson must get in the habit of writing.

Writing will increase your authority.

Below are seven benefits I attribute to writing on a daily basis:

1. *Writing will make you a better salesperson.* Effective writers often write like they speak. For sellers, a great deal of that writing is focused on selling an idea or even a specific tactic. Working on clearly stating ideas in writing will improve your ability to quickly articulate them in a selling or interview setting. Your writing practice will allow you to build up a reserve bank of pretested discussion points.

2. *Writing will make you a better thinker.* In order to create content that is succinct, reveals new ways to look at ordinary things, or applies simple solutions to seemingly complex problems, you must think about your business and your customers much differently. Far too often, we go with the accepted norm in business. When you begin to break ideas down in an effort to write about them, you may find yourself questioning the norm and stretching yourself to include new thinking.

3. *Writing will make you a better listener.* When you engage in conversations or listen to radio interviews, you'll start to listen with a writer's ear. You won't just listen to the content as it's presented. Often, you'll find your head filling up with ideas for blog posts by listening to others discuss even unrelated subjects.

4. *Writing will make you a better speaker.* This one develops nicely from the previous point. When you start working through blog posts on meatier topics, the ones that readers weigh in on, you will begin to create and then refine better presentation ideas and material. Just the fact that you research what others have written, flesh out examples from your own experience, and discover tools and tactics unrelated to what your organization offers will give you a much deeper well to draw from as you develop your presentations.

5. *Writing will keep you focused on learning.* The discipline required to create interesting content requires that you stay on top of what's hot and new, and on what's being said (and not being said) in order to find ways to apply it to your specific sales and customer environment.

6. *Writing will allow you to create bigger ideas.* The habit of producing content will eventually afford you the opportunity to create larger editorial ideas that can be reshaped and repurposed for other settings. Eventually you will be able to take a collection of blog posts on a specific topic and turn it into ebooks and workshops over and over again.

7. *Writing will establish your name.* When you can point to articles published in third-party publications, guest blog posts run on popular industry sites, quotes in journals read by your prospects and customers, and reviews of your ideas shared on your blog, you will experience a competitive advantage in the market that few can match. Your writing will change the context of the selling environment.

I urge you to consider these factors if you think you don't have the time or the reason to write. It's crucial that you do.

How to Become a More Productive Writer

You might note that the title of this section doesn't mention becoming a *better* writer. Here's what I know: if you become a more productive writer, if you start to see the benefit of consistently sharing your ideas through your writing, you'll become a better writer.

So, first let's work on making you a more productive writer.

Become a better reader—You might have guessed this one was coming, but it's a fact. Reading blogs, business books, magazines, and even content that is not necessarily linked to your particular area of business or personal interest will help you find your own style and voice more than any other activity.

As Stephen King said, "If you don't have time to read, you don't have the time (or the tools) to write. Simple as that."

Keep a swipe file—When you read, bookmark material that grabs your attention. It may be because of a certain style, a certain lack of adverbs, or a lyrical use of certain words. No matter the reason, you need to start putting things away for a rainy day. You never know when you'll come up empty for topics or just need to revisit some great writing to get you in the right frame of mind for writing. I also find that I get one idea here and another there. Sometimes my best posts come from combining seemingly disparate ideas.

You can bookmark good content using plastic file folders for physical documents or employing a tool like Evernote to digitally clip, organize, and store examples.

Keep an idea file—Using an online outlining tool such as WorkFlowy, or a simple notebook, store and then access ideas as they come to you. Since you know you'll need more content later this week or later this month, just keep adding ideas as what you read gives you flashes of insight. One day, you'll be stumped on what your next article or post should be, or you'll need inspiration to plan your week of blog posts. At that time, this list can help you push out of an idea block.

Be opinionated—You don't have to anger people with your writing, but you don't have to agree with everyone either. One of the ways to be more productive in your writing is to respond to industry trends, accepted ideas, and any given week's hot topic with a view that's counter to the crowd. You should take a stand you can defend, of course, but explaining your own view on the day's popular issues can provide a lot of fodder for posts, articles, and more.

Write like you talk—I think this is just good advice, no matter what. It's easier to write in your own voice, and you extend your personality to the reader more effectively by just being who you are. People who don't write a great deal sometimes start to think too much about others actually reading their writing. To combat the self-consciousness, they tense up and focus on sounding smart, using bigger words, or writing in a more academic way. The result is usually stiff and awkward.

You want your writing to retain your personality. If you were an English major known for turning a poetic phrase, then by all means, write in that manner. If, however, you're a straight shooter who's at her best when calling it like she sees it, then don't mince words!

Stay organized—One of the most effective ways to increase your writing productivity is through outlines. You were probably taught this in grade school, but the lesson holds true: if you are organized in your thinking, you'll write faster and more clearly.

There's nothing harder than sitting down and composing seven hundred words with no idea of where you're headed. Decide on your main point, then create three to five subheads and three to five bullet points per subhead. Your specific outline may differ, but this is the most effective way to write quickly.

Used a timed method—Set a timer on your computer for forty-five minutes (I use Apimac Timer) and write with your head down until the bell goes off. Then get up and do something else for about fifteen minutes. I find that this approach makes me feel more motivated to write, even when I'm working on a very long piece. I work more deliberately if I know there's a set time for a break. This tactic also allows me time to focus, clear my head, and then come back with renewed energy.

Let it rip—Don't stop every ten words or so and revisit what you wrote. Just get the content down on paper or in a file first. You can go back and fix mistakes and errors later, but try to get the first draft done before you do too much to fix it.

Edit sober—For this point, I draw from a famous Ernest Hemingway quote: "Write drunk, edit sober."

You don't have to take this literally, but the idea of coming back to your writing after a cooling-off period is a good one. It's pretty tough to assess the quality of your writing, let alone address omitted words, when you're in the throes of brilliant ideas. In a perfect world, I would let anything I write rest for a day, but when you're up against a deadline, any amount of time away from your work is helpful. Give yourself a time-out, complete another task on your to-do list, and then come back and take another look at your writing.

Spend the most time on the title—My last piece of advice has more to do with getting more readers than increasing productivity, but if you spend extra time on any element of your writing, spend time on the headline or title.

There's nothing that makes your writing more productive than the impact of more readers!

Beyond the Single Use

Now that we are fully engaged in the act of writing to build authority and establish credibility and expertise, it's time to expand your thinking in ways that allow you to extend every piece of content you create.

Don't worry—this doesn't always have to mean more writing. One of the great skills of the inbound marketer is repurposing and adapting content for multiple uses. The sales guide who uses inbound marketing techniques can use this skill as well.

For this idea to pay off, you must develop a mentality that automatically considers every word you publish or plan to publish to be part of a giant Erector Set of content that can be used and reused in many ways.

Every blog post, press release, video, article, and presentation must have intended uses beyond its obvious initial use. Each piece should be an interchangeable element in the total body of work. It's simply too costly to produce content any other way.

I once had a conversation with Josh Waitzkin, eight-time national chess champion and author of *The Art of Learning*. He told me that he had gotten to the point in his career where he no longer saw a chess match as it was; to him, the game always looked the way it would look many moves ahead.

I think that's how content must be viewed. Not as how it appears now, but as moves to come. The process starts with asking yourself this line of questions—questions that should evolve into an unconscious way of thinking.

- How could I expand this blog post into a series of posts?
- How could I rework this content into other formats?
- What would make this content worth paying for?
- How could this content be reworked for real-time consumption?
- What did I learn while creating this presentation?
- How could I package this content to share it with a different market?
- If I were writing a book, would this content belong in that book?
- What content have I already written that could form the basis of an ebook?
- How can I share this content in a way that helps me learn?

Below are five content development habits that you should employ in the creation of your content strategy and in the production of your body of work.

New Purpose

If you are asked to present a specific topic to a group, do the following: create or develop your thoughts for a series of slides, write a blog post or two from your research, record a screencast of the presentation, upload your slides to SlideShare, and have the video transcribed into text.

There is very little additional work on your part, but with this small effort you can create four or five pieces of content by discovering what to include in a ninety-minute talk.

New Form

I've produced dozens of ebooks over the last few years, and all of the content for these compilations has been drawn from my blog posts. Now, understand that this doesn't happen by chance; I deliberately plan it that way.

Organize and write your blog posts with possible ebooks in mind. This requires a more involved strategy in approaching both blog post topics and the chosen topics for ebooks, but when you understand that the long view is required, it's actually quite freeing.

As we discussed in chapter seven's Total Content System, getting in the habit of creating an editorial calendar in advance, with your cornerstone topics always in mind, can be a great aid.

New Medium

One of the most puzzling aspects of content is consumption—how people choose to get, read, listen to, watch, or otherwise digest information. Understanding that people have distinct preferences opens the door to an interesting aspect of repurposing.

I have a podcast that's free to subscribe to, but hundreds of people have paid $2.99 to download the Duct Tape Marketing podcast app from iTunes because of the added control it gives them. Some people value the fact that they can locate all the shows in one place and easily track the ones they've listened to. People consume content in different ways and you should position yourself to add value on *their* terms.

Don't always assume that people want to consume content the way you've chosen to deliver it. Figure out every possible angle of consumption and meet as many of them as possible.

New Time Frame

This one can be a bit mind-bending for some, but you have to think about real time and the long term in the same context.

As you write something that you think is interesting or tweetable, push it out to Twitter even before you finish it, then again as you write things that you're wrestling with yourself over. There's something very powerful about involving followers in the writing process. You may find that you can work out some new thinking based on their input and engagement. People consume this content in a far different manner than they do a full blog post, but the engagement is incredibly instructional.

Social media is the ultimate real-time content feedback loop, and this is how you tap it.

New Audience

Blog readers and newsletter subscribers often compose two very different groups for salespeople. Sure, there's some crossover, but some people prefer e-mail newsletters while others won't read anything that's not in their RSS reader. When you understand this, you can begin to explore various methods of reaching people in their preferred environment.

Giving away content in the form of a free ebook is a great way to reach new audiences, as is creating workshops and making them available as Udemy courses and reworking your ten all-time best blog posts and offering them as guest posts on other blogs.

Once you start to think in this vein, you'll never look at a blog post or PowerPoint deck in the same way again.

Speaking for Leads

Speaking, in an effort to persuade, is what the act of selling is all about.

While many sales professionals are often gifted communicators, few think of themselves as speakers in the traditional sense. But one of the greatest ways to establish yourself as an authority in your industry is to routinely present at industry conferences, trade shows, and panels. Back before radio, TV, and certainly before online platforms, the best orator won the argument, the election, and the sale.

While you may never come to consider yourself an orator of any stripe, there's a good chance you need to use the spoken word to convince and convert.

I'm suggesting that you proactively take this practice up a notch and add public speaking to the mix as a way to build authority, demonstrate expertise, and increase your sales efficiency.

Okay, authority and expertise you probably buy, but efficiency?

Think of it this way: when you're asked to present your ideas, one client or prospect at a time, you can get in front of ten people a day, that is, if you're operating at breakneck speed. But one well-thought-out presentation might put you in front of several hundred qualified leads. In speaking to crowds, a half hour speech can result in hundreds of people simultaneously knowing who you are, liking what you have to say, and trusting that you know a thing or two about your business. It doesn't get more efficient than that.

Get to the Podium

What would it mean to your bottom line if every time you got up in front of a prospect or a group of prospects, more and more of them became clients, referred you to other prospects, and asked you speak to their groups?

Speaking for leads is a very useful strategy for getting your expert message in front of many potential customers at once. Don't think of it as public speaking—think of it as sharing your authority with a whole host of prospects in person.

Here are five tips to make your speaking pay off big.

1. *Get referred:* One of my favorite strategies is to approach two potential groups and offer to present great information to their clients and networks. The key here is that you have a topic that is very hot and seen as very valuable. This is not a sales presentation; it's a way to educate and add value to people who might not necessarily know about your workshop events.

    Approach two partners with the idea that you'll run a workshop or give a speech on a great topic that they can offer to their customers and cross-promote to each other's attendees as part of the deal.

You simply get referred in as the expert. (Every time you do this, you will likely get asked to speak at an event one of the attendees is involved in as well.)

2. *Make a deal with the sponsor*: Even if you've never been paid to speak at an event, you still have valuable information to present. Remembering this: you should be willing to waive your speaking fee, but only if the organizers allow you to tell the audience that you have products and services you can offer them beyond the speech. You should also be allowed to reveal that you'll be offering some freebies in exchange for contact information.

   Make it known that you have no intention of selling these further products or services from the stage—you're merely informing the audience of their existence. This approach raises the value of your presentation and gets you what you need in a lead-generation opportunity. But tread with caution: if you overpromote, don't expect to get asked back.

3. *Educate like crazy:* Don't be afraid to give away all your secrets in your speeches. Some suggest you should just tell the audience what they need, but not how to get it done. I don't agree. If you tell them how to get something done, some may think they can do it themselves. But those who really want what you have (and those who you want as clients) will realize through your specific details, how-tos, and examples that you do indeed possess the knowledge and tools to help them get what they want. Educate and you won't have to sell!

4. *Collect those addresses:* People will sometimes rush up to you after a thought-provoking presentation and ask how they can buy your products or services. Make sure you give all attendees a valuable reason to share their contact information for the purpose of following up. You can offer them the slides to your presentation, a free resource guide related to your topic, or a more detailed report based on the topic, all in exchange for business cards. If you don't have this pre-planned, you'll find you won't get a second chance to wow them.

   I hope it goes without saying that you should also have a follow-up process. Send a handwritten note to interested prospects, add them to a prewritten drip e-mail campaign on the topic, or call them up after the event to measure their engagement.

5. *Include a call to action:* When I first began speaking, I would present highly useful information to the participants, being mindful not to overtly sell. When the speech came to an end, there would be an awkward moment when I knew people wanted to buy something I'd talked about, but I didn't have an offer.

I quickly learned that the lack of an offer didn't serve either of us very well. If you provide great information and a clear road map to solve someone's problems, you'll often find they want you to reveal how they can take the next step. Here's the key—in that environment, they want a deal they can act on right away. Not every audience or speaking engagement will present this opportunity, but I've found that in a free speaking gig, where I've been given permission to introduce my products and services, this three-step approach is well received:

- Tell your audience right up front that at the end of the presentation you're going to give them great information about what you do.
- About halfway through, after you've built up trust, take a quick minute to reveal, say, a paid workshop or program you have coming up. Name the price, and then move on.
- At the end of the speech, answer questions, make free offers, and then, almost as an afterthought, agree to let participants bring a friend to the event you mentioned (at the same price) if they sign up for it today. You've just made the event half price in their minds, turned them into recruiters, and given your potential attendees a valuable tool to offer to a friend or colleague. Anyone considering the offer is now highly motivated to follow up. Don't hard-sell this—simply put it out there and let people do the math. You want to avoid tainting your wonderful information with a sales pitch, but don't leave those who want to buy without an option either.

Become a More Effective Speaker

Of course it's not enough simply to get to a podium. The goal is to communicate in a way that educates and inspires. While public speaking and presenting in a selling environment have some things in common, there are many things that effective speakers need to learn in order to create the greatest impact and establish their authority.

Many people struggle with speaking in front of an audience. The only real cure for this is to get up and do it, realize that no one suffers permanently from nerves, and then get up and do it again.

There are three bits of advice that I would give to anyone desiring to become a more effective and authoritative speaker. For me, this means getting your point across in a way that inspires listeners to do what you want them to do.

Share the love: One of the most important elements an effective speaker brings to an audience is passion. This can be passion for helping people get something valuable from hearing the advice presented or passion for the subject itself. You can't fake passion, but when you have it, your message often comes through clearly regardless of the polish of your speaking style.

If you're naturally passionate about your subject or the purpose of your speech, don't hold back—let people be attracted to that passion. If, however, your position requires you to present information that may be useful, but doesn't exactly capture your imagination, then your job is to inject something you *are* passionate about. Let's say you are talking about network security, but what you really love is World of Warcraft, music, or baseball. I believe you will become a much more compelling speaker when you find a way to weave topics you are passionate about into your presentations.

Become a TEDhead: The TED (Technology, Entertainment, Design) conference, as many of you know, is a worldwide phenomenon that pulls in speakers with "ideas worth spreading." TED is one of the best resources you can use to become a better speaker.

TED speakers are chosen because they are fascinating and because they have passion for a big idea. The format challenges them to present that idea within eighteen minutes; most use very little in the way of slides or media. Every TED talk is recorded and then housed on the speaker's site. The most popular ones get millions of views.

Make the TED site your classroom and you will have access to a tremendous collection of speakers who will inspire you and teach you how to be better speaker. Watch everything they do. (I recommend starting with Daniel Pink's talk on the science of motivation.)

Shoot your free throws: Legend has it that Larry Bird, the great NBA star, shot one hundred free throws every day, even after he became a superstar. He also led the league in successful free-throw shooting year after year. He didn't stop practicing just because he was good.

To be a better speaker, you've got to practice. You may choose to spend a lot of time in front of a mirror going over your presentation, but I suggest you get in some pickup games pretty quickly too.

Find a Toastmasters chapter in your area and force yourself to present and then receive critical review from a peer group. Seek out opportunities to present your ideas wherever you can. Speaking to the knitting club's monthly lunch may not get you in front of the audience you ultimately desire, but it will get you live feedback and help you get better.

Another thing about practicing in front of an audience is that it almost always leads to other speaking opportunities.

Create Better Presentations

There's an art to making good presentations. Unfortunately, in the world of really bad presentations, it can be hard to figure out how to do it right. You've probably sat through numerous presentations that featured speakers reading off slide after slide of impossibly small bullet points.

Don't be that person. Bad presentations are a waste of everyone's time and often are a product of laziness rather than incompetence.

The way to make a good presentation is to keep your audience in mind as you create a reasonable argument for whatever it is you want them to know. Do you want your audience to be entertained or do you want them to understand a complex topic? Figure out your goal before you start and stay focused on that. Below are a few steps that I take in creating my presentations:

Start "analog": Like most people, I used to fire up PowerPoint and start churning out slide after slide, with no initial planning. The problem with this approach is that you don't see and feel the entire picture; you only get small chunks.

Start in analog mode, with a giant whiteboard and several packs of sticky notes. Outline the entire map of your presentation; add, subtract, and rearrange ideas before you ever commit anything to presentation software. Only after you're done with that are you ready to move on to creating the actual slides. And note that while desktop presentation software like PowerPoint and Keynote are the norm, growing numbers of presenters are moving to online collaborative tools like SlideRocket and Prezi.

Think about the journey: Many people come to hear a presentation because they need to learn something or because they've been asked to consider a new idea. This may mean they come to the presentation with some internal resistance.

A great presentation addresses people where they are now, transports them to a world of new knowledge, points out the roadblocks and challenges along the way, and helps them alter their perceptions so they can use the information presented to them to change their world. People need to believe that they can *use* the information you present, or it won't matter how good it is.

This is why great presentations end logically with a call to action.

Tell your story: Great presentations have a lot in common with great cinema in their storytelling. Stories are often told to entertain, but the use of stories in presentations, even when just reporting information, can help to dynamically illustrate even the most complex of ideas.

Mixing client success stories with information is how you create desire and drama. Telling stories moves people and makes them want to adopt your point of view. Presenting in a narrative format also makes information more digestible.

Great presenters draw upon personal stories and borrow heavily from the story lines and structure they find in movies, as well as in literature and mythology.

Remember that less is more: Many slide presentations consist of little more than read-along notes and would be just as effective delivered via e-mail! I could write pages on this crime alone; suffice it to say that your slides should be used as visual clues to amplify your message, not to tell it.

Set up your slides so that they help viewers remember a key point. Try to reduce the content on your slides to one word or one image that reinforces that point rather than teaches it from scratch. Strip a concept down to one quotable (and tweetable) phrase and use that for dramatic impact.

You should use your slides as a tool, not as a crutch. And remember to practice with your slides; your presentation should glide along with your words. In many cases, you can create notes for yourself and view them, rather than your slides, on the computer screen, using it like a teleprompter.

Keep a presenter's mind-set: Much of the fear that surrounds public speaking is rooted in the fear of being judged. "People won't think I'm smart, good, funny," and so on.

While you might have been asked to make a presentation because you did some unique research, wrote a killer blog post, or have expertise in a subject, the real reason you are there is to help people come to their own understanding of the information. You're more like a mentor than a guru.

There are two books that every presenter—or anyone charged with creating presentations—should read. *Resonate: Present Visual Stories That Transform Audiences* and *Slide:ology*, both by Nancy Duarte, are the one-two punch that will teach you everything you need to know about crafting and presenting your ideas in ways that will make your message matter.

Another great place to find example presentations—good, bad, and in a class of their own—is SlideShare, the online presentation hosting service that makes it very easy for you to post and embed your presentations on websites. You can search by specific topics to find examples and templates of others' presentations.

Beyond PowerPoint

Most presentations are given by a speaker standing in front of a bunch of people and lecturing them for thirty minutes or so, right?

Well, it doesn't have to be that way. One of the skills good speakers eventually master is the skill of engagement. Sometimes the best way to get an idea across is to let your audience think it's their idea. A little back-and-forth can go a long way in shaping how an idea, and the presenter of that idea, is accepted.

The following five approaches can act as idea starters for your next presentation.

Question me this: Imagine showing up to present to a group and instead of lecturing them, you divide the audience into groups of five or six and task each group with quickly creating a list of questions around the proposed topic. You can then build your presentation as a series of responses to the core questions that come from each group.

Draw on the right side: I once attended a presentation on retail displays during which the presenter handed out art supplies and had each participant draw or craft an example of a great display unit for a fictitious new product they were launching. He then worked through three or four of the displays and broke down what was good and bad about each one. It was a fascinating learning experience and the participants were highly engaged with the presentation's creative element.

Collective collaboration: What would happen if you posed five very relevant questions or five challenges, then split the audience into groups and asked them to use their collective expertise to suggest, synthesize, and present a solution to their respective question? Although this is the opposite of the first approach I recommend, it does just as much to get the audience fully engaged in the process.

Break a case: Taking a cue from the traditional business school case study, present your group with a challenge in the form of a case study (or multiple case studies, for a large group). Ask individuals to present their solutions or recommendations to the group.

Ask Google: Break your audience into small groups and give each one a problem or task that they need to research online for ten minutes. Then apply the collective wisdom of the online world to a problem in near real time.

I know that each of these presentation approaches involves its own set of logistical considerations, but imagine how engaged groups could be if they learned from one another while you, the presenter, facilitated and provided relative insight—instead of another slide deck.

Virtual speaking

Finally, a speaking engagement doesn't have to mean bringing a group of people together in a room somewhere. Today, there is plenty of inexpensive technology available that makes it very easy to present to a group of people online.

Online seminars (or webinars, as they are often called) have become commonplace, and they offer lots of benefits. You can use services such as MeetingBurner, GoToWebinar, or AnyMeeting to set up and host your own online educational sessions for one to one thousand participants. These systems also have built-in sign-up and lead capture as well as automatic reminders.

Any and all of the methods outlined throughout this chapter can be incorporated into an online event with a high degree of success. And many participants may prefer the online format, as it doesn't require them to leave their offices to attend.

GOOGLE+ HANGOUTS ON AIR

I want to dive deeper into one platform in particular because I think it offers some pretty attractive benefits: ease of use, no cost, and automatic, high-quality archiving.

The Google+ live video chat function, Hangouts, has been around for a few years. However, with the addition of Google+ Hangout On Air with

YouTube, which allows you to broadcast and record your Hangout to your YouTube channel, Google+ Hangouts became a much more valuable sales and marketing tool.

The opportunity to create and record engaging video content is tremendously simple with this tool. Whether you want to do one-on-one interviews or host an industry panel discussion featuring ten experts, Google+ Hangouts On Air gives you a live streaming platform and automatic HD video capture.

I love the immediacy of a live broadcast, but this program also gives you the option to edit the final version in YouTube. That way, you can take out slower moments, edit out questions, or punch up the broadcast with an intro or images. You can use it for many different formats, including:

- One-on-one interviews for a video blog post
- Peer-to-peer industry discussions
- Preconference or event showcases
- Opinion or current-event discussions
- Survey data analysis and discussions
- Live customer case studies or success profiles
- Product launches
- Educational seminars

Partner and Facilitate

The final component required to make your content platform and authority efforts even more potent is to use what you've built to build up others.

You've taken the time to put all the listening, content, and authority-building elements into place, so why not use your newfound skills and knowledge to help build your own strategic-partner team or network?

One of the best ways to network for referrals is to develop a team of like-minded individuals or companies that see referring and introducing you and your insights as a way to add value to their client relationships.

I believe this is one of the most powerful sales concepts out there. Yet most salespeople misfire on this concept because they see it simply a way to prospect for referrals.

If you want to change the context of selling, then consider building strategic-partner teams into your model. Think about the possibilities. What if you used your content platform to build and lead a team of other highly motivated salespeople or companies? What if you used the authority you've gained by following some or all of the tactics outlined in this book to create a strategic advantage with your highly select team?

There are a number of components involved in the creation of an effective partner program.

Recruit and introduce: The first step is to recruit your team and introduce them to your team concept and business. Ask your current customers to name other businesses or salespeople they like to work with and buy from. You don't want just anyone as a partner; these should be people you can also confidently refer business to.

Next, send these potential partners a letter outlining your plans and inviting them to tell you the best way to introduce their business to your customers.

Create content opportunities: Invite your partners to contribute to your newsletter or appear as a guest on your podcast or blog. Giving your partners exposure by way of content helps them get their word out and provides you with even more content. You can even take this up a notch by creating a group blog optimized for all of the partners.

Conduct video interviews: Set up a meeting with your partners and use the opportunity to record an introduction video. By letting the world know about your partners, you're letting other prospective partners know that you intend to exchange value.

Acquire special offers: As a way to enhance your offering, get your partners to contribute a product or service: free business cards for every logo purchased or free flowers when you make a reservation for dinner, free tickets to a show, or a free HVAC checkup when you have plumbing work done. This is a great way to promote your partners while adding real appeal to your marketing.

Make referrals: Make it a habit to go out of your way to refer business to your partners. Don't wait for people to ask; do it as part of your Monday routine. By consciously making referrals, you become someone great providers want to partner with. You also increase your value to your customers by consistently helping them get what they need in every aspect of their lives.

Rate and review: If at all possible, become a customer of every one of your partners. This will make you a much more authentic referral source (as a user) and allow you to test and filter truly great experiences. Follow up on this by actively writing reviews and assigning ratings on Yelp and other online sites.

Create events: Figure out how to bring your partners together to network and create deeper engagement. Let each partner have a day when he or she educates everyone else in the network. Create workshops and offer to conduct them for your partners' customers. Develop an educational day or workshop devoted to topics that each of your partners can present. Give all partners a one-hour presentation slot and have them share their expertise and information. Each of the presenting companies can then promote the event to their own communities in an effort to build attendance for the entire day.

Speaking, writing, and publicly sharing high-value content in the places where your prospects go to find information is how you build the kind of personal authority that creates awareness and allows you to stand far out in front of your competition.

Today's prospect is looking for people who can add value—and the breadth of your content footprint and authority-building efforts are how you get found before others even know a prospect is looking.

CHAPTER 10

Mine Networks

For years, salespeople have pounded the pavement, literally and figuratively, looking for prospects. These days, because you can reach almost anyone, it's not about how many people you can blindly reach, but how you efficiently and smartly mine your networks and make the important connections.

It's critical that you develop the habit of proactively mining networks to find opportunities long before a prospect even starts looking for a solution. You must use social networks to go deeper into the organizations you serve by building stakeholder maps based on network connections.

You need to take advantage of the ability to accelerate the velocity of deals by zeroing in on opportunities that are moving in real time.

Social Media in Sales

Smart salespeople have learned to tap the power of social media, but unfortunately, many companies still see social media tools and their associated networks as a pointless, even scary place for their sales teams to focus on.

And many salespeople don't fully understand the power of social networks in the sales process or, at best, they relegate it to the role of a digital prospecting tool.

It's amazing to me that this mentality persists. I realize that there is potential for confusion if sales reps are left "out in the wild" to create their own messages and brand assets, but the downside of restraining (or disregarding) the powerful opportunity offered by social media is far greater.

Today's qualified prospect is often far easier to find and reach using social channels.

Today's prospect often shares invaluable buying signals and data via social channels.

My first job out of college was a sales job, and I recall my first sales mentor: my father, coaching me on ways to scan a prospect's office for clues that might provide conversation starters and common ground. Things like diplomas, photos, and awards were the data points for relationship building.

Today this data, as well as information about buying patterns, challenges, company culture, and news that may affect purchasing needs, is often shared freely in social networks.

There's a familiar saying that's often applied to the world of business: "It's not what you know, it's who you know." The rise of social sharing in the sales environment has transformed this equation to: "It's not who you know, it's what you know about who you know."

While the process of sales may always involve face-to-face education and persuasion, many elements of prospecting, relationship building, and value adding can be greatly aided through the consistent use of social media.

Jill Rowley, head of social selling for Oracle, identified four components of social selling, all enabled by technology:

- Networking
- Research
- Relationship building
- Distribution and sharing of content

She is teaching Oracle's twenty-thousand-plus sales pros how to use social networks like LinkedIn and Twitter to find their buyers, to listen and relate to them, to connect and engage, and to influence their buyers' online ecosystems. Rowley says the goal is to socially surround the buyer, the buying committee, and the third-party thought leaders, experts, consultants, and partners who influence that buyer.

Sharing content is a great way to engage your buyers. Read what your buyers read and share that content across your social networks.

Follow the 4-1-1 rule. Share four pieces of third-party thought leadership content for every single piece of company-branded content, then throw in a cat picture. Okay, it doesn't really have to be a picture of a cat, but it should be something light and inspiring—a motivational quote or a TED talk.

Mining

Blending social media data into CRM systems has become commonplace in the sales environment, but smart salespeople are taking it much deeper by mining social networks to develop and save searches related to their products and services.

When a potential customer complains on Twitter about a faulty product or asks about something related to a business or personal need—and you're paying close attention to just that kind of tweet—you might have just found an open invitation to start a conversation with a prospect.

I'll get into some best practices by network in a bit, but first let's re-check your basic listening tools. Many of them are great starting places for mining data as well.

Your lead-mining toolbox should include:

Twilerts—a service that sends you alerts via e-mail when terms you've selected, based on the kinds of things you know prospects talk about, are used on Twitter.

Talkwalker Alerts—a free service that sends alerts, based on your chosen search terms, when they are used in a blog post or news release and indexed by Google.

HootSuite—a free app that allows you to monitor Twitter for search terms and follow selected lists of Twitter users.

Feedly—a free tool that allows you to subscribe to and read RSS feeds. By subscribing to the blogs and news feeds of prospects' companies, you can scan for important nuggets. I also use the Reeder app on my phone to easily scan and share content when I'm away from my computer.

Connecting

Mining social networks is only part of the equation. Social networks are all about connecting and, in many cases, discovering who is connected to whom. Research tools such as InsideView and SalesLoft can unlock potential opportunities for connection.

Change is good. Job changes offer a number of opportunities because they can involve a cascade of changes due to a move at companies A and B. Your contact now has a new position. The person he replaced probably moved somewhere else. The person who replaced your contact in his old position is now a prospect and that person probably left a job at another company, thereby opening up yet another connection you can engage with!

So you see, while change can create a little crisis, it can also open doors—if you go after all four of these changes immediately.

Engaging

A great deal of energy in relationship building is focused on getting and closing the deal. As most sales professionals know, however, the long-term money is in growing relationships before and after the sale. This is where loyalty, repeat purchases, and referrals happen.

The changing world of sales has in some ways become more complicated and in other ways more open, but one thing will likely never change—the sales professional who consistently finds ways to offer more value will win.

Socially enabled tools for content sharing, filtering, and curating shine in developing that long-term engagement. One of the best ways to establish increased value is to provide value in ways that may be, or at least seem to be, unrelated to the products and services you offer.

I believe that some service providers are being chosen these days based on their ability to find and share the good stuff in addition to making sense of the changing stuff.

Your engagement toolbox might include:

- Using your Feedly reader to create industry-specific feeds
- Using tools such as Storify or Scoop.it to create custom topic pages
- Using Q&A sites like Quora to home in on key industry challenges

Adding Depth

Another essential mining skill is the ability to go deeper inside the organizations you serve or hope to serve. How many accounts have been lost over the years because the salesperson had a great relationship with the buyer, only to see that buyer move on to another company?

By mining social networks for a bigger view of your buyer's world, you can start to build other relationships inside the organization and uncover potential new opportunities. If you've built an advocate in your original relationship, you may find that this approach makes it easier for her to open doors for you rather than simply asking her to make a referral. Likewise, it may not make sense for you to build a relationship with your contact's boss's boss, but it may be a very smart play for you to connect your boss's boss with that person.

Social networks like LinkedIn are very good at revealing connections between individuals as well as highlighting the basis of the connection. This information can become valuable as you begin to work on a targeted prospect.

Another very important reason for going deeper into organizations is to understand how a deal really happens. Have you ever had one of those deals where, just when everything seemed to be going great—your client was all thumbs-up and talking about getting the PO ready to go—the process ground to a halt and then eventually faded away?

Chances are the deal was killed by stakeholders you were not aware of—and the bigger the organization, the more stakeholders are involved. If you're selling a software solution to a purchasing department, there's a really good chance that IT, Sales, Operations, and maybe even Finance are going to have a say in the who, what, when, and where of the deal.

You can use social networks to construct company stakeholder maps and start connecting with and understanding the IT department as actors crucial to the sales journey. This doesn't mean you're going to start pitching everyone in the organization, but there's a good chance that you can actually help your buyer understand the real buying process better when you take this kind research approach. (That sounds like adding value and insight, doesn't it?)

Now let's turn to a handful of best practices for mining the current major social networks. To some degree, your ideal-client profile and industry will help dictate which network might make the most sense for you to go into most deeply. For example, if your primary focus is B2B sales, then LinkedIn is the place. If you sell an especially visual service, such as home remodeling, then Facebook and Pinterest might be fertile grounds for your mining efforts.

LinkedIn Best Practices

LinkedIn is not the biggest social network, but when it comes to connecting with people who mean business, no other social site can compare.

A study conducted by HubSpot in early 2012 suggested that LinkedIn is 277 percent more effective for lead generation than Facebook and Twitter combined. The professional decision maker audience that prefers LinkedIn is much more prepared to participate in the kind of traditional, authentic networking that leads to lasting business relationships than any other audience.

Salespeople and recruiters know that LinkedIn is the place to go to prospect. I would like to suggest that it can be a great deal more than that. Below are some ways to get the most out of LinkedIn.

Get a paid account: A paid LinkedIn account will cost you about the same as a client lunch, but with this comes the ability to connect more easily, send e-mail directly to people, know when people have viewed your profile, build prospect lists, and track things such as job changes.

There's even a professional-sales level of service called the Sales Navigator that includes higher levels of key prospecting and connecting tools.

Join Groups: The power tool on LinkedIn is Groups. For me, this is the closest thing to the proven offline networking groups that exists online today. Groups can give you access to people and discussions related to an industry, topic, or even geographic region. Working LinkedIn Groups effectively is a solid way to build a network and generate leads.

Currently, LinkedIn allows basic members to join up to fifty groups. Find industry, topic, and location-specific groups that contain concentrations of people you would like to network with and join them. Spend time looking at the level of participation and conversations. If all you find is updates, with members promoting their businesses, move on; that group will be of little benefit to you.

LinkedIn has a useful "groups you may like" function that suggests groups based on your current profile and connections. See what kind of groups this search leads you to.

Also, note that the best groups for lead generation on LinkedIn are those that don't tolerate blatant self-promotion. Find those—and don't self-promote.

Connect with members: When you join a group, reach out with a very brief introduction, telling why you joined the group.

Look for active members and add relevant replies to a number of posts. This starts the process of initiating one-on-one conversations. Because your replies are publicly available to all group members, you can use this technique to demonstrate that you have a lot to offer.

Once you've joined a group, you have a common connection with every group member. LinkedIn helps by allowing you to connect with people in that group based on your mutual group membership. It's a little thing, but it's a step beyond simply saying you want to connect blindly.

Don't, and I repeat, don't simply send connection requests with the default (but stunningly bland) "Because you're a person I trust, I would like to add you to my network." Seriously? I can't think of anything closer to spam than that. If you really want to connect in a meaningful way— the only way that this is going to pay off in the end—take the time to write a genuine note with some personalization. Tell the recipient what you're working on, why you want to connect, what you've recently read—anything that might make him stop and think, "This person seems interesting!"

Here's what Jill Rowley, social media evangelist for Oracle, advises the thousands of sales reps she trains. There's an art to creating a compelling LinkedIn invite. Personalize your invitations. Try something like this: "Jill, thank you so much for sharing your perspective on personalized selling. I learned X, Y, and Z. I would be honored to be in your network and delighted to have you in mine."

As I was writing this section, I thought I would check my own LinkedIn account, just for grins. I had nine link invitations waiting, and all nine had the same default message. It's just not that hard to stand out by doing the simple things that few others are doing.

Create your own groups: Once you get the hang of Groups, you should consider creating your own topic group. This is not a company or product group; it's a group that is set up to discuss a particular topic that your prospects, customers, partners, and even competitors might find worthwhile.

To come up with a topic, consider talking to a group of clients to see what they would be interested in discussing with others in their industry or position. Here's a place where mining frequent questions and discussions on a site like Quora might turn up some ideas.

Add starter content that gets people talking. Participate in conversations. Promote. And above all, do not tolerate spam and self-promotion. Tell people you intend to take a strong line on that. Give them one warning if they break the rule, then kick any offenders out. If you don't set this tone from the very beginning, your group members won't want to stick around.

To get the most from your group-manager role, create a landing page on your own website that promotes the idea behind the group and encourages visitors to join. This will deepen your connection to the group and help people better understand what the group is all about.

Finally, use, but don't abuse the "announcements" function. As a group manager, you can send direct announcements to all group members via e-mail. This is a great way to continue to keep your group and its activity front and center.

A word of warning on forming groups: if you want your group to grow and give you the ability to benefit by virtue of your status as the group's manager, you have to commit to spending the time to curate and moderate the group and to stimulating and facilitating group participation.

Reach out: Once you start to get more active on LinkedIn, make it a habit to reach out to five connections each week, with the sole purpose of saying hi, thanking them for their participation, congratulating them on a promotion, checking in with what they've been working on, and so on.

Smart salespeople have done this in the offline world with handwritten notes for years. As they will tell you, the impact of reaching out personally is dramatic and long lasting.

I can't tell you how often this personal touch leads to business, even though that was not the intention. It's amazing how relationships bloom when you genuinely care about people.

Facebook Best Practices

Facebook is the biggest of the social networks and has a decidedly different feel than LinkedIn. If LinkedIn is like a chamber of commerce networking event, Facebook is more like the world's biggest happy hour.

Business is done on Facebook, but it's done in a different way. While people turn to LinkedIn to network and find deals, people turn to Facebook to have fun; deals sort of accidently come about by way of relationships. Although Facebook is a network and networks are a sales-person's friend, you have to play by the rules of the network's culture if you expect your participation to pay off in the long run.

The benefit of Facebook over other networks is that if you gain a high level of engagement with fans and friends, you can enjoy the added ben-efit of exposure to their networks as well. The key, in my opinion, is to spend what precious time you have for networking on Facebook focused on drawing conversations out of a smaller, but fully engaged, group.

Below are a handful of practices that can help you do that.

Focus on the wall: This one still confuses some people. Most fans and friends don't actually visit your page; they engage or read updates in their news feed. In many cases, then, adding all kinds of tabs and pages can be for naught. Focus your time on interacting within your own news feed and adding content to your wall.

Enable public subscribers: While many people still use Facebook as a somewhat private network, it gives you the ability to post content on your personal profile and then allow public subscribers to see it. I've seen a tremendous increase in engagement on personal profiles used primarily for business since this feature came along. Many people use their per-sonal profile for both business and personal use; this action effectively lifts the five-thousand-friend limit and allows you to share content with public subscribers who are not listed as friends.

Add photos directly: Most people will tell you that photos do very well in terms of level of engagement, and that's true. One tactic that increases your engagement is to add your blog posts and then share a photo with the post. So, instead of simply posting the link, which would add the im-age from the post as a thumbnail, you add the image directly to Facebook and then add the link and description. At the time of this writing, these posts are being shown by Facebook to a larger percentage of your fans.

Build interest lists: A lesser-known tool on Facebook is Interest Lists. Anyone can build lists that others can subscribe to, or use this function privately to organize pages without having to "like" them. (Think of how you could build a competitor interest list with this tool.) It's like an RSS feed of a group of Facebook users. You can build some engaging lists around topics and draw people in to subscribe, but you can also scroll just through the updates of your list members instead of wading through the entire Facebook news feed to easily interact with this filtered group. One of the well-worn tactics for getting more engagement on your own wall is to engage others authentically on their walls.

Consider a customer group: Facebook also allows members to create groups. Depending upon the niche you are in and how many of your customers use Facebook, this could be a great way for you to facilitate customer interaction. Groups can be public, invite-only, or completely private (meaning only people you add can see anything that happens in the group). This can be a powerful way to help customers and have customers help one another, and can create a feeling of community among your best customers. But, before you charge down this path, make sure to think about whether or not a customer group would add value. Just because you can do something doesn't always mean you should.

Use Facebook Advertising: Facebook offers a number of interesting advertising options. As with all advertising, Facebook Advertising is designed to attract people to content and information, not to sell them. Your marketing department should have overall brand and product advertising covered, so I only suggest this tactic as a way to increase your authority and to mine networks more deeply.

The best approach is to promote content that draws people into your network. When you write a blog post, schedule a webinar, or have a hot ebook to give away, consider promoting your posts using the Facebook Sponsored Posts option. That way you can drive e-mail signups and "likes" based on people interested in your specific topic, for very little money. You can exclusively target fans and followers of your top competitors, allowing your ads to be extremely dialed in.

Twitter Best Practices

While Twitter tops 500 million users, it's still probably one of the networks most underutilized by sales professionals.

Taken alone, Twitter can seem like a pretty mindless waste of time—more notable for getting celebrities in trouble than building sales muscle. However, when you consider the major objectives we've been discussing in this book—sharing, linking, networking, listening, building expertise and authority, and amplifying content—Twitter has some things to like.

Below are the best practices for using Twitter as a selling tool:

Follow wisely: There are really only two things you need to do on Twitter: read what others have to say and hope that people read what you have to say—in your allotted 140 characters.

Many people think the name of the game is getting lots of followers and following lots of people. There *is* a correlation between following and being followed, but the first order of business on Twitter is to figure out how to make it useful. Having many followers may feel like a primary goal, but usefulness is the true goal of anything you spend time on.

Follow your customers, industry influencers, competitors, and the journalists who write about your business. As your starting point, you can also add a few lists others have built. Don't worry about the rest at first.

From this group, Twitter recommends people to follow based on your current follows, and you can see who follows whom. This is how you expand your connections wisely—by mapping networks, starting with your prospects and customers.

Build lists: Once you start to follow any number of people, it gets pretty hard to pay attention to nuggets they might share without spending a great deal of time scanning through Twitter. That's not a good thing.

Use the Twitter list feature to break your groups into manageable subgroups. One of the primary lists, for example, will be your customers. Create your lists, then use a tool such as HootSuite to add your lists as columns so you can easily view, share, respond to, and message each group's members and tweets.

Share daily: Over time, one of the most beneficial things you can do on Twitter is share other people's content. Yes, you'll want to tweet your latest blog post, but you should also get in the habit of tweeting ten or twelve other pieces of content or updates. Again, think useful; don't just mindlessly retweet everything your customer shares. Any followers you have acquired will appreciate the fact that you are sharing useful content from others and the people whose content you share will appreciate it as well.

Expand your sharing to include your RSS feed of blogs each day as well. HootSuite and Buffer both allow you to schedule ("buffer") your tweets so that you can do your morning reading and then schedule your shares to appear throughout the day.

Set up smart searches: Twitter has a powerful search function that makes it easy to find prospects. Go to twitter.com/search and play around with the many ways to sort, filter, and search. You can find businesses in Michigan complaining about their server being down again, cloud storage not working in Texas, printers acting up in Idaho, or the lack of a comprehensive HR strategy in Florida. Or you might hear them asking if anyone knows a good web designer, programmer, or writer anywhere in the world. All of these cries for help might spell opportunity for the business listening in real time.

The point is, people turn to Twitter to ask for help, source products, and get advice. By creating and monitoring searches that signal the kinds of requests that are related to your business, you might easily turn up leads.

Google+ Best Practices

So far, Google+ has taken a backseat to other networks with all but the most Internet-enthused and those in tech-related fields. For this reason, though, I believe Google+ holds some hidden opportunities.

The key to making Google+ pay is to think about it as a way to make additional connections in your key constituent groups—customers, suppliers, partners, and industry influencers.

There's no need here to think in terms of building the largest network; think instead about building a strategically broad and deep network where it counts. Create circles that contain the obvious suspects. Then start searching for active Google+ Communities to participate in. Not all communities are active (or valuable), so you may have to look harder to find communities that are both relevant and worth your attention.

Below are some Google+ practices that will make your time spent there profitable.

Link your authorship: As stated in an earlier chapter, linking the content you publish on the Web with your Google+ profile may indeed be the best reason of all to participate on Google+. Do not pass go until you do this! Think about the opportunity for social proof when a prospect goes out there searching for a solution and finds your content, along with your picture and your Google+ profile, on page one of the search results.

Create smart circles: Google+ is naturally built around custom groups called circles; for obvious reasons, your first circle should include your customers. Here again, if your customer is active on Google+, whom does he interact with the most? This can also be a great way to find new connections and new content to share on other platforms; people who are active on Google+ are often less active in other networks. Make sure to share and to "+1" on their content as well, since Google pays close attention to the interaction on Google+ when it comes to a more complete view of search.

Dig for communities worth joining: Google+ has a group tool called Communities. Anyone can create and moderate a community; some are very active. Look for communities related to your industry and join a few that seem to have a fair amount of engagement. Communities work best when there's an active moderator stirring the pot and asking for input. Many communities are little more than parking lots for abandoned spam, so take a good look before jumping in.

Get good at Hangouts: I've talked about this one previously, but I can't say enough about the current opportunity to stand out from the crowd using Google+ Hangouts. This is essentially a group video chat with enough bells and whistles to turn it into a low-budget TV station. The ability to stream live as well as record your Hangouts opens up so many content possibilities. And since it's a Google service, Hangouts archives can rank very well in search.

Getting Links

Another, somewhat unexpected way to mine networks is to think of the entire Web as one big network—which is what it actually is. Sometimes networks need to find you, and not the other way around. That process starts when someone links to your site or to some piece of content you've placed in a social network.

Links back to your site from other sites send Google and, for that matter, anyone looking a potentially important signal: "Hey, I'm a human being and I think this is good stuff." That's something Google can't do with its algorithm, so it relies on real people to tell it, by way of a link to the content in a blog post or on Google+, if this is quality content. It's even better if Google already considers the site in question to be a trusted source of valuable content.

Links have always been important, but in the past, the focus was on getting lots of them. The "more is more" approach led to gaming and buying and other unnatural types of acts. SEO folks and site owners seemed more concerned about getting links than producing anything worth actually linking to and visiting.

Link building in the age of authority has more in common with effective networking than magic SEO art. Viewed in this light, networking for links is a great way for an individual salesperson to enhance both her reputation and her authority, not to mention her search results.

Below are tactics proven to effectively build (and then continue to build) high-quality, relevant links.

One word of caution: none of these tactics supplants the need to be "linkworthy" and none involves tricks of any kind. You draw high-quality, relevant links the same way you develop networking relationships—by focusing on the needs of your link partners and your readers.

Snack-sized influence: One of the best ways to get some very high-authority links (and this includes RTs, +1s, and "likes" from high-authority people recognized by Google) is to publish quotes, advice, and answers from influencers in your industry.

The key to getting content from influencers is to make it as easy as possible for them to provide it in snack-sized bites, as we explored before. Ask one question, for example, of a dozen people, publish the answers in a thought-provoking post, and link to each participant's site.

Often this approach will produce a high-quality, or at least interesting, piece of content that others, including your influential guests, may think worthy of linking to and socializing.

Guest content: As I've already mentioned, one of the highest-quality links you can get is a link back to your site from the body of a blog post on an influential blog. Hop over to a service like Topsy to do a search on your "key terms + guest" and find yourself some great opportunities to draw links from your guest content.

There are two potent variations on this theme. First, you can *ask others to write a post on your site.* You can get some tremendous content and, as likely as not, they will link to that content once it's published. And second, *interview guests for a podcast.* Authors love to do this around their book launches and many influential people in your industry may want to do the same. More often than not, your guest will link to this content.

Promote an event: Events are another great way to draw links. If you or your organization hosts an in-person workshop or even an online seminar, you can likely attract links by listing your event on local event pages such as Meetup and Eventful.

In some cases, you can get some pretty terrific links from the event space. Imagine hosting a free talk at the public library in your community. You'd probably get high-domain authority links from local media calendars and the library's .org link.

Your partners: Getting links from your partners is yet another reason to work hard at establishing a formal strategic-partner network.

In a way, this is the updated version of the linking networks that were in vogue before Google slapped them down. The big difference is that these should be, by virtue of how you build them, far more natural.

Build something useful: Want to know the easiest, fastest, most productive way to draw tons of links? Create a highly useful free tool and tell people about it. People love to find and share stuff that's useful and, of course, it's even better if it's free.

One of the most linked-to pages on my site is for a free press release generator called Instant Press Release that I created years ago. The tool also generates hundreds of newsletter sign-ups each month, even though I never do anything to promote it.

It is worth investing in having something built. Look to your organization for some existing resources such as calculators and proof-of-concept models that might be adapted for this use.

Real-world networks: What organizations do you belong to? What alumni organizations? What business groups? What nonprofit boards or committees? These may not seem like great places to get high-traffic links, but they can often be highly industry relevant and carry high-authority signals for Google.

I realize that most of the options above require real work, but Google has stated, loud and clear, that the days of buying links in farms are over. Keep creating great content, sharing great content, and building your own authority. Networking and links—the kind that won't ever go out of fashion—will follow.

Making Introductions

Many of the practices outlined in this chapter revolve around mining networks with an eye to expanding your connections and going deeper into your customers' networks. Once you establish contacts this way, you'll want to find ways to deliver tangible assets as a result of all the networking.

In that regard, few things deliver networking ROI faster than a proactive habit of making introductions.

What would happen if you took your new listening, networking, and mining skills and began introducing customers to other suppliers because you saw they had a need? Think of the possibilities: introducing prospects to journalists because you heard a journalist was looking to interview someone in his industry, introducing two or more strategic partners to each other because it was obvious they would hit it off, pairing members of your IT team to members of a client's IT team to work on a shared issue. Could this practice add value and differentiate you from the pack? Is it possible that just thinking this way could change the way you thought about social networks?

Introductions are networking gold. In fact, the right introduction can be far more powerful than the typical referral, and there's a right way and wrong way to make them.

We've all been in a conversation where a friend or colleague will say, "Hey, you should meet John." Next thing you know, you get an e-mail that says "Suzy, meet John. John, meet Suzy. You two take it from here."

Now don't get me wrong, people appreciate the introduction. But now both of them have to figure out how to have a conversation—or whether they even really want to have one. There is a better way to introduce people to one another.

I was having one of those brainstorming conversations with a friend when I mentioned that I was interested in writing for a particular magazine. He said he knew someone I should meet, and proceeded to send us both what I think just might be the perfect introduction e-mail (details changed to respect privacy).

John,

By way of this e-mail, I'd like to introduce you to my friend Gary Smith.

Gary is an expert on how to build partnerships with the media. Currently he leads Media Buzz and recently came out with his latest book, How to Land PR by the Truckload. In addition, he played a key role in helping me start Effective Financial Planning, my coaching company for financial advisors. He's very interested in leveraging his talents to build a higher profile as well as an information marketing solution.

For more background see landPR.com.

So, in one paragraph he:

- introduced the person
- detailed his expertise and credentials
- explained how they knew each other
- explained what the person was looking for

Then he added the same about me, enabling us quickly to establish who the other was, why we might have a conversation, and, at least initially, what we might talk about.

This approach is such a useful way to make an introduction, and it adds value to both parties. It even offers a call to action at the close.

If you take the time to make thoughtful introductions, you will increase the value you bring to every interaction.

Build Your Own Leads Group

Leads groups have been around for quite some time. They differ from networking in that they are about passing active leads to members of the group, but there's still a huge element of networking that goes on in leads groups.

There are many formal leads networks, such as Business Network International (BNI), and many informal local breakfast groups that offer the opportunity for business owners to build their businesses via lead sharing. Perhaps you belong to one currently, or have in the past.

Leads groups can be very powerful for generating sales leads, but a complaint you often hear is that some groups work and some don't, depending upon the makeup of the group. Many traditional groups require a big commitment in terms of time and meetings. It's hard to control the quantity and quality of the leads.

My advice to sales professionals is to take the best from what works and build your own leads network. Below you'll find some tips on making your leads group pay.

Handpick your team: This is one of the most important steps and it should start with your current customers. You can build a best-of-class team for your leads group by asking your current customers what companies and individuals they like to do business with and most often refer. By doing so you can find team members who come recommended and whom you already have a common bond with.

Create a map of all of your current clients' products and services needs and look to fill your leads group with ten to fifteen businesses and individuals who fit into that list.

Set goals and expectations: One of the things that formal leads groups do well is set rules and regulations. While I think that's important to get established right up front, your selection process might be more important.

As you select team members, paint a picture of how you see the group operating. Discuss goals and expectations, for example, how often you'll meet and what people need to do to stay active.

Integrate technology: One of the downfalls with current traditional groups is meeting requirements. Some groups require ninety minutes every week, with stiff penalties for missing meetings.

Technology can take away a great deal of the need to meet as frequently face to face. I think it's still important to do so, but you should employ a tool like Localbase or Loops from passingleads.com to help facilitate lead sharing, tracking, and scoring. That way, people can share and track leads in real time and easily measure and analyze the ultimate contribution of every member of the group.

Create opportunities: Another way to make your leads group stand out is to think beyond pure lead sharing and expand into the area of creating opportunities for the entire group. Once you have your group members all sorted out, why not look into ways to create content-sharing opportunities such as a group blog or the creation of an ebook listing all the group members that the entire group can pass around to their customer base.

Think about ways that your group members could work together to create online and offline events or offer special discounts, product samples, and gift certificates for services for one another.

Meet up: Make sure that you keep the "in real life" aspect of your local group alive by meeting at least once a month to share leads and expand upon ideas to grow the group. You might even consider asking group members to invite potential members to these meetings.

Another powerful way to enhance your monthly meetings is to turn them into networking events as well, so that members of the leads group can invite and meet prospective clients.

The control that this approach gives you also allows you to create the feel of the group that really suits your way of doing business. If you like to have wine at your leads group, go for it. If you want to give your group a fun or educational feel, meet in interesting locations around town each month.

Creating and controlling a group like this further establishes your credibility and can raise your profile in the community—in other words, create authority as well as leads.

Coselling

I want to wrap up this discussion of lead mining by introducing an entirely different approach to bringing leads into your Hourglass. You may recall from chapter six that the first step in the Marketing Hourglass is awareness, or the "know" stage.

One of the greatest ways to create awareness and referrals is to mine other people's networks. In other words, give people a reason and the motivation to introduce you to their customers and prospects by way of what I call coselling (or perhaps comining).

Coselling, or getting others to actively mine for you, isn't a new concept, but surprisingly few people do it. The basic idea behind coselling is to form a small network of best-of-class providers who can act as an additional arm of prospecting for one another.

I've seen this done with remarkable results—sometimes tripling and quintupling the number of leads an organization creates—particularly for businesses that operate on a local level.

How to Set It Up

Approach a number of your customers and ask them to share the names of other companies they love to do business with. You may already know some of them or have an idea whom you would like to partner with, but I find that if you can dig up a few shared connections—your mutual customers—it makes the idea take off even faster.

From this group, pick four or five at the most and propose meeting to discuss cross-promoting one another's business.

The key is to find a logical way to make it easy for one another's salespeople or technicians to comine in a way that makes sense to the customer. I find that in some cases the best approach is simply to ask a customer with whom you are doing business if he has any other needs that might be served by one of your trusted partners.

In many cases, the client will be grateful that you can refer someone. He'll be even more grateful when you're able to give him a coupon or gift certificate to use with that supplier.

While you'll want all participants to pull their own weight, don't keep score. Also, I encourage you to avoid paying referral fees, to add incentives such as coupons and discounts, and to create a packet of information that makes it easy for each participating business to leave promotional materials for all the partners.

Think about the power of this approach. If today you're able to make twenty sales calls in a day, tomorrow you and your partners might make one hundred a day. Think that could add some impact to your sales?

Here are some examples that illustrate the concept of comarketing in action.

Graphic design: Customers of a graphic designer's are probably using services like printing, website design, promotional-item sales, and copywriting.

A graphic designer could offer every customer who needs identity work five hundred free business cards, a free website audit, one free sales letter, and one hundred free pens (with updated logo) as part of a new-customer package.

This not only creates exposure for the partners, it really sweetens the deal for the graphic designer.

Insurance sales: I've included this one because insurance salespeople get a bad rap—they're selling something we hope we never have to use.

The ones who succeed understand this and they know that their real job is to bring value to their clients in as many ways as possible. If an insurance salesperson can develop trusted relationships with people who bring accounting, planning, marketing, and legal expertise to small-business owners, they'll dramatically up their value. By becoming a bit of an expert in all of these areas, as they relate to small business, the insurance salesperson can develop his or her reputation as someone who "gets" small business, not as someone selling something we don't want to need.

Plumbing contractor: Any business that goes into the home to do repair will always find home owners receptive to referrals from other trusted providers. The plumber should have a comarketing relationship with HVAC, window cleaning, electrical, carpet, garage door, fencing, landscaping, and roofing suppliers at a minimum and leave behind that "little black book" of trusted suppliers every time one of their salespeople or technicians calls on a customer.

Wedding photographer: Weddings are an ecosystem of sorts. They offer a perfect opportunity for comarketing because there's a very known and logical progression of needs that comes with a wedding. Basically every wedding photographer knows that his or her customers will also need a florist, baker, invitation designer, caterer, event facility, tailor, and gown shop.

Now, you won't always fit in the right order of things in every situation, but once you've earned the trust of the couple and their parents you'll be doing them a huge favor if you can recommend other vendors.

Comarketing is a powerful referral-generation tool that can be employed with very little cost and can result in even deeper customer relationships.

CHAPTER 11

Build Your Sales Hourglass

Prospects have gotten very good at figuring out solutions to their obvious problems, thanks to access to the unprecedented amount of information available online. Salespeople can no longer provide solutions to obvious problems. What they need to do now is help prospects understand their not-so-obvious problems, the ones they may not even realize they need to solve.

Customers need salespeople who can lead them on a journey through what I call the Sales Hourglass. I'll explain exactly what the Sales Hourglass is, but first let me explain why the journey is essential.

Today's sales professional needs to be good at understanding and building cases for problems that the market doesn't yet know exist. This is a skill that comes from helping customers think bigger and from understanding exactly how your ideal customer makes a buying decision. It's important to have a sales methodology or approach that's infused with a greater understanding of the customer, as we have covered so thoroughly in this book.

Today's sales process must be bathed in collaboration.

The idea of a "sales process" is not new. Most salespeople, at some point in their careers, either are trained in or figure out a system that becomes their de facto method, or process, to move a lead from inquiry to close.

A sales process is really little more than a standardized set of steps that a salesperson follows in order to create consistency in what he or she offers a client.

The most common sales approach goes something like this: a prospect demonstrates interest, the salesperson digs for pain, presents a solution, handles objections, proposes a purchase, wrestles with terms, handles more objections, then goes in for the close.

Some firms have embraced a more adaptive approach, one that zeroes in on understanding and controlling the buying process itself—how a buying decision is made, what selection criteria are used, how benefits are quantified, and, most important, how funding for the purchase is allocated.

An alternative to either of these approaches is to be the organization or individual who defines the problem to begin with. Rather than winning the fight for "why choose us?" how about controlling the fight for "why choose anything?"

As we discussed in part I, adding value is a large part of the work you're engaged in. To a great degree, your ability to add value depends on your capacity to codefine what constitutes value in the eye of every prospect you encounter. In other words, you must personalize your organization's value proposition with your prospects and clients on a case-by-case basis.

What I'm describing constitutes a somewhat dramatic shift in the context of the sales process.

The Sales Hourglass takes a completely different view of selling than simply walking your customer from initial contact to close. This new view really is about leading prospects and customers on a journey they didn't even know they intended to make. That's not to say that we will suggest they go somewhere else, or buy something that's not right for them; quite the opposite. We are going to make sure they arrive at the most helpful destination of all. That's best done when we view our job as journeying with a prospect or customer instead of simply leading them or, worse, following them to where they say they want to go.

Perhaps this would be a good time to reemphasize the extreme significance of building your authority and expertise, as we explored in chapter eight. To a large degree, the effort put forth in that phase is what elevates your stature to the point where you gain permission to hold these higher diagnostic conversations when you're ready to actively step into the sales process with a client.

Make Problems Visible

In a report on vendor research, Forrester Research reported that 65 percent of vendors who create the buying vision during these early stages get the deal. In other words, if you can help a prospect shape the problem and participate in defining the parameters that solve the problem, there's a good chance you can make yourself the only one who can design the perfect solution.

As I was working on this book, I read an article in *The New Yorker* by Dr. Atul Gwande, author of *The Checklist Manifesto*. In "Slow Ideas," he describes how some ideas, innovations, and solutions catch on quickly while others take years to catch on and spread, if at all.

Gwande cites the example of two medical advancements—the development of anesthesia and sterilizing operating rooms and equipment—that were introduced at about the same time. One was adopted globally in a matter of months, while the other took decades to be commonly adopted.

In less than a year from its introduction, the use of anesthesia became a standard medical practice. The use of procedures needed to keep operating rooms sterile, on the other hand, took more than twenty-five years to take hold widely. From "Slow Ideas":

So what were the key differences? First, one combatted a visible and immediate problem (pain); the other combatted an invisible problem (germs) whose effects wouldn't be manifest until well after the operation. Second, although both made life better for patients, only one made life better for doctors. Anesthesia changed surgery from a brutal, time-pressured assault on a shrieking patient to a quiet, considered procedure. Listerism [a sterilizing practice], by contrast, required the operator to work in a shower of carbolic acid. Even low dilutions burned the surgeons' hands. You can imagine why Lister's crusade might have been a tough sell. This has been the pattern of many important but stalled ideas. They attack problems that are big but, to most people, invisible; and making them work can be tedious, if not outright painful.

So often, solution selling attacks problems that aren't obvious or simple, or the attacks are on problems that people don't really want solved.

The key to success in the adoption of anesthesia in the example above resided in the fact that the problem was clearly visible and the solution was easy to adopt.

So, how can you make problems visible? How can you be the one who crafts the buying vision?

Make Solutions Easy

Perhaps the most frustrating moment for salespeople is when the buyer simply does nothing to proceed in the buying process. They don't go with a cheaper price, a better widget, or a more established player; they just decide to do nothing.

The bigger the deal, and the more established the company looking to buy, the bigger an issue this becomes.

Think back on your own buying habits, and see what usually stops you from making a decision on a purchase. My guess is it's one of about three common deal busters. You're either not convinced something will work, you fear the risk of change is too high, or the proposed solution seems complicated.

The longer a buyer has been in the game of buying solutions, the more she's been proven right on these fears—things *don't* work as promised, the cost to switch *wasn't* worth the benefit, and nobody will use the new software because it's just *too hard* to get people to change their habits.

The key to moving buyers away from these states is to help them make problems visible and quantifiable and work to build solutions with them.

Remember, Teaching Sells

One of the biggest reasons I insist that you write, speak, and educate as an expert is because these practices will better equip you to find problems that your clients might not even know exist—and make them visible.

The experience of digging around in your industry (or your client's) with an eye to teaching what you find will help you develop the key skill of collaborative selling, a skill that is based on a much higher level of on-going feedback, which you receive when you present new findings.

The practice of teaching will also help you craft the appropriate message for each audience of stakeholders or levels within an organization.

The Sales Hourglass Defined

When I introduced the Marketing Hourglass earlier in this book, I noted that there would be a Sales Hourglass as well. In many ways, the two Hourglass applications share the same concept: guiding a prospect or client along a path or on a journey.

In the Marketing Hourglass, the journey creates the opportunity. A prospect first comes to know about your firm or solution and then moves, in many cases unguided, through a series of intentional steps designed to instill belief, which leads to the trust required to actually engage a firm.

Traditionally the middle of the Marketing Hourglass—the try and buy phases—is where the sales team steps in. As I've suggested repeatedly, the job of sales professionals today is to insert themselves in the buying process earlier, and stay with it longer, so that they can personalize the journey before, during, and after the sale.

The shape of the Hourglass draws upon the notion that the job of sales is much broader in the phases prior to and after a sale and only gets more narrowly focused during the try and buy phases required to make a sale.

The Sales Hourglass, then, is a set path that a salesperson, in conjunction with marketing, can use to help a prospect become engaged in the specific process of buying.

The key difference between the two Hourglass applications is that while the Marketing Hourglass is broadly focused on an ideal-client persona or description, the Sales Hourglass is focused on an individual prospect or need and operates on a much more personal level.

Another core difference is that the journey through the Sales Hourglass must be based on the mutual understanding that you and the buyer are prepared to determine that there may be no journey after all. The Sales Hourglass might not lead to a closing—and that destination is okay too. Contrary to what your sales manager may want, not every prospect is a good fit. Sometimes getting to "no" quickly is just as useful as struggling through "maybe" indefinitely.

Think of the Sales Hourglass as your individual-prospect playbook, the tool that will help you tailor your sales method for each client. One of the greatest benefits of a structured tool such as this one is that it keeps you focused on the next step, even if that next step is the decision to pursue other opportunities.

Merely introducing the Sales Hourglass to a prospect will allow you to stand out as it introduces valuable steps not often taken by traditional sales professionals. Your prospects will find value in knowing you are using a system to dig deeper into identifying the right problem. The Sales Hourglass process (or whatever you decide to call it) is in itself a valuable teaching tool. I believe that these steps demonstrate not only a better way to sell, but also a better way to buy.

As you read through the next few pages, you might start to wonder how you will access some of the information and insight you'll need to guide your prospect. Before we go deeply into the stages of the Sales Hourglass, I recommend that you review the section on deconstructing community from chapter two. As you recall, there we introduced a process that would allow you to go deeply into an organization and uncover the roots of its operational DNA—its community. Draw upon that work as you begin to tailor your Sales Hourglass approach with each prospective client.

The logical steps of the Sales Hourglass are as follows (I've placed the steps from the Marketing Hourglass within parentheses alongside each step to highlight their somewhat parallel paths):

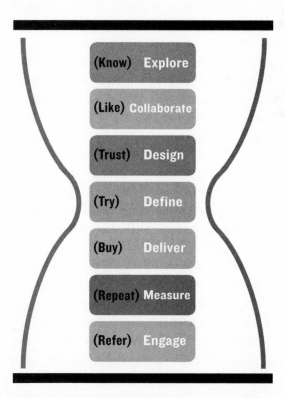

Explore (Know)

The *explore phase* is where you'll conduct your own research—discovering the elements of community, constructing stakeholder maps, and uncovering problems that you can make visible.

This step can begin in response to a sales request, but it must not be conducted simply as a response; rather, it is an opportunity to explore the best possible solution or path for a prospect, even if that path differs from or contests their stated directive.

I know this advice may sound brash, but once you develop the habit of obtaining a deep knowledge of your prospect's business, you must use that knowledge to push him to think bigger, teach him new things, and provide him with insights into how he can be more successful. You can't do that by merely responding to what he says he needs and then working to build a close personal relationship. However, you may find that you develop closer personal relationships with your clients when you deliver this kind of value.

Not everyone will want to hear what you have to say. That's okay—that's the point. The exploration step taken in this fashion will make you more important to the clients who appreciate value and will definitely make you more of an asset to your organization.

Here's something to keep in mind: a great deal of what I've shared in this book will require some exploration with other members of your sales team, your sales managers, and the marketing department. You'd better get comfortable with pushing people on new ideas, because you'll be doing it a lot in this new sales process.

Collaborate (Like)

The next step in the Sales Hourglass is to take what you've learned in the exploration stage and start talking with a prospect about innovations.

At this point, you're just discussing bigger-picture ideas, but don't be surprised if you start finding out things that your organization doesn't want to hear. Things like, "I need your products to do X" or "Why can't anyone figure out how to solve Y?" But simply asking for and receiving this kind of information will make you more valuable to your clients and to your organization. (I intend to keep repeating this point!) Once you start bringing new ideas from your discussions with customers back to product development and marketing, don't be surprised if the CMO or CEO wants to have a regular chat with you from time to time.

The *collaboration phase* starts with encouraging the prospect to dream about what she needs, determining what the underlying problems are, and imagining what the world would look like if her problems were solved. This brainstorming doesn't mean she'll be able to give you the right answers, but it's a start.

This phase also consists of sketching ideas (and possible solutions) that perhaps don't yet exist and getting a prospect to think about how these ideas might affect his success. This process takes guts, because the best possible outcome might *not* be available through you. But I believe the long-term game is always best served when you deliver value, no matter what the package.

Design (Trust)

The next step is to begin designing a solution with your customer and with your company based on the specific challenges your initial steps turned up. I know this might sound suspect if you've come up in a world driven by a catalog and inventory levels, but winning in today's sales environment requires creating custom solutions that reach beyond a set of specs. Push customers to think beyond rigid solutions to see new ways to use technology, social sharing, and collaboration as innovations that can move them forward.

If you sell products, think about a solution that turns your product into a service. If you sell services, focus on ways to use your service to help evolve your customer's business model into a more collaborative shape.

Imagine if you expanded your thinking from "this is all I have to sell" to "anything is possible" in terms of creating a successful customer journey. When you open up your thinking in this way, you may find that you can more easily spot opportunities and challenges and explore innovative ways to suggest change.

Define (Try)

Once you've effectively crafted a solution with and for your prospect, turn toward defining how the solution will be structured, delivered, implemented, and paid for. This step essentially is where you offer a proposal and, if you've carefully executed the preceding steps, this is where the deal is inked. Because the design of the solution is a collaboration, there is no active or aggressive closing involved. The customer essentially accepts a reality he or she helped to create.

This is not to suggest there won't be a great deal more work to do. Perhaps the solution you cocreated needs a sponsor to gain budget, maybe many more stakeholders need to weigh in on and understand the implications of this new approach, and perhaps even your primary contact may begin to question certain elements of the overall vision. The beauty of this step, however, is that you've essentially excluded direct competitors from the mix.

The *define phase* also signals the end of the collaboration cycle and keeps the momentum of the project moving toward the designed outcome.

Deliver (Buy)

In many organizations, once a deal is inked, the salesperson's job is done. Customer service, project teams, or delivery experts take over. There are many good, practical reasons for this kind of handoff, sure. But I believe the true expansion of your value comes from staying very active with the client in some manner.

This may very well require extra time and effort on your part, yet it's crucial to your success. If you and your client started this journey together, you're probably better equipped than anyone else to make sure you either end up at the destination together or take side trips that make sense.

At the very least design (in conjunction with your marketing department) an orientation process that allows you to elegantly move the process to other team members or departments.

If you want to build a reputation for delivering value, you can't ever abdicate the progress of the journey.

Measure (Repeat)

Quite often, the value of a solution can't be easily measured, and yet it's essential that value be assigned. The Sales Hourglass performance operates at a much higher level when you become obsessed with measuring, analyzing, and communicating the value your customers receive.

This might mean that you get permission to work with individuals and departments beyond your buyer in an effort to help them quantify the tangible results they've received. You may have to interview users, tabulate surveys, observe operations, and dig into some data in order to measure the actual results. The impact of being seen as a salesperson who cares that results were realized is invaluable.

There are many positive outcomes from taking this course. You can discover instances in which a client did not receive what she expected. If you can discover any shortcomings and see that they are addressed, your reputation for delivering value will soar. Measuring results also means you will surely discover instances in which a client received extreme value—and you can use this knowledge both to cement loyalty with your existing customer and attract new ones. Just understanding the relationship between measurable value and cost will make you much better prepared to have confident discussions with prospects regarding pricing issues.

You may also discover instances in which your client received exactly what he expected. Helping your client actualize these results reinforces the value of working with you, leads to additional positive contacts, and opens the door for additional opportunities.

Engage (Refer)

It's amazing how often sales professionals neglect to engage past customers until it's time to reorder or time to review a contract. Frequently reengaging customers is what leads to the discovery of new opportunities, new introductions, and referrals.

The beauty of delivering amazing value before, during, and after the transaction is that you'll be seen not as a pesky salesperson checking in, but as a valued contributor or consultant the company is eager to do business with again and again.

The Sales Hourglass is a powerful sales methodology, but it does not need to be viewed as a process strictly employed by the sales department. The Sales Hourglass is also a teaching process and can be equally effective in the hands of the business development, customer service, technical support, and HR departments. In fact, many firms could benefit from using this methodology with internal stakeholders to create more collaborative buy-in for things like new technology deployment and annual priority setting.

Begin with the End in Mind

Here is a suggestion that might help keep you focused on the right approach as you begin to formulate your thinking around your Sales Hourglass.

When businesses create a new product or service offering, they usually begin by developing the attributes of the product or service. Makes sense: you don't have anything to sell unless you create something people want to buy.

The very next thing they do, once they think they have a winner of their hands, is go to work on the promotion of the new offering: the sales letter, sales pitch, and brochure. Every salesperson I've ever worked with on the Hourglass framework takes the same line: once they understand the prospect, they go to work on ideas that will create awareness and build trust.

All great and necessary considerations; but I would like to suggest taking a much stronger path.

The very first thing you should think about in creating your Sales Hourglass is what you want the customer to think, say, and feel about your product or service 180 days after they make the purchase. Then, work backward toward the point where they become interested in making a purchase. In other words, determine how you are going engage a customer after they become a customer, *before* you start thinking about getting an appointment.

The processes, touches, and follow-ups you'll have to build by taking the "customer experience" approach will ensure that you have a winning sales process, promote a winning product or service, and thrill your customer with a winning experience (and capture referrals).

In the rush to create and promote our goods, it's this final, crucial point that often goes without thought or is made only after repeat sales and referrals lag. I'll say this again and again: the sale is not complete until the customer is so happy that he or she confidently makes referrals.

With this in mind, let's look at a "begin with the end in mind" process for a software solution you're promoting. It might look something like this:

180 days after purchase—The customer receives free updates and an offer to meet with a select group of other users in an invitation-only peer-to-peer group accountability program.

90 days after purchase—The customer receives an e-mail offering him 30 percent off any other product or service of his choice as a current customer courtesy.

60 days after purchase—The customer receives a coupon offering a free evaluation of his progress with the training course and the opportunity to engage a consultant to help him if he is stuck working on his own.

30 days after purchase—The customer receives a coupon for a free sixty-minute coaching session to help keep him on track.

14 days after purchase—The customer receives a coupon for thirty days of unlimited e-mail support to keep him on track with his purchase.

7 days after purchase—The customer receives a mailing, with additional bonus materials, as a way of thanking him for his purchase.

Immediately upon purchase—With a successful transaction, the customer is directed to a Web page where a welcome video tells him when and how he will receive his purchase. Automated e-mail provides instructions and orients the customer to the contents of his new purchase and provides details on how to receive support if he has questions.

Trial—After viewing the video series, the prospect is offered the opportunity to receive a free thirty-minute coaching session to discuss his specific challenges.

Information gathering—After the seminar, the prospect is offered the opportunity to sign up to receive a video series of client case studies and an ebook featuring content covered in the seminar.

Awareness—The prospect attends an informational online seminar that dives into the problems most businesses face when trying to find the solutions that your software addresses.

Here's what you must do to make this step even more powerful: envision the Hourglass turned upside down. Make referral generation the *first* thing you consider. Ask yourself this question before moving on: How will I get every single one of my clients excited about introducing me to other prospective clients?

When you start designing this process with the referral in front, you'll be forced to focus on the things that matter most to the client—the experience, the follow-up, the results—and not on the things that matter most to you. Superstars keep that point of view firmly fixed in their minds.

CHAPTER 12

Finish the Sale

A sale is not a "finished" sale until the customer receives a result.

Of course, this assumes you've helped your client quantify what a good result is. Part of the journey should be focused on understanding the objectives your customer is trying to achieve and measure as a result of your product or service.

Because you're now well acquainted with the Sales Hourglass, you know that you have to stay involved in the customer's experience before, during, and after the commitment or sale is made. Staying connected in this manner is also how you get more referrals and better understand the needs of a client going forward.

The following processes need to be considered as part of your standard selling procedure and should become a necessary part of finishing each and every sale.

Review Results

One of the most potent things you can do as a salesperson is quantify delivered results. It's how value is often measured.

A results review is one of the key components in the *measure and engage* stages of your Sales Hourglass. Now, the actual results a customer gets from what they've purchased may rely on factors far beyond your control, but staying connected to the customer experience in ways that allow you to monitor and measure results should be part of your deal with a customer.

It doesn't matter if you rely on or are compensated for repeat sales from each customer or not. If your customers aren't getting results and realizing value, you won't get referrals!

If fact, tell the customer that you intend to stay connected and set the expectation for a follow-up process to review results. Make a point of being involved in the start-up or introductory process when your organization begins to provide the contracted service or delivers the product you've sold.

The great thing about committing to this level of involvement after the sale is that there are only three things that can happen, and each of these possibilities can lead to further positive engagement.

1. *The customer gets a bad result*: Let's say you follow up and the client didn't feel that things went as she expected. I know this isn't what you want to hear, but hear it you must. Now you can go to work fixing the problem.

    Without a process in place to circle back and measure results or satisfaction, your client just drifts away and stops returning your e-mails when you reach out to touch base with her later on. However, when you give a client the opportunity and the space to talk about a problem, she gives you the power to become a hero by fixing or shining a light on the problem.

    Unfortunately, many salespeople run from this approach because their companies don't really want them to intervene. Or maybe you simply don't want to hear your customer's complaints. As troubling as mistakes and challenges are, they give you an opportunity to prove your value. By paying close attention to where things go wrong, you can help your organization get better while increasing your value to your customer.

2. *The customer gets what he expected*: While this may not seem like cause to jump up and down and celebrate, if the result the customer receives is representative of the result other customers of your organization often receive, then you'll want to dig in and find tangible measures of the impact.

When you can put a number on the benefits of doing business with your organization or on the solution you and client composed, you'll build a foundation upon which to base your future projects. When you know, for example, that most clients realize five or ten times the value over their investment, you'll speak to these results often and won't feel any pressure to avoid pricing conversations. If your product reduced labor costs by 20 percent, for example, that's a number you can use!

3. *The customer gets far more than she expected*: Obviously this is the kind of result everyone is hoping for. By proactively seeking it out, you can make sure you're ready to seize the potent opportunity it presents.

A client who has an exceptional experience quite often looks for ways to tell others about her success and your role in it. This is your opportunity to provide testimonials and case studies to the customer, at the very least. It may also present a natural moment to explore referrals—either internally to other departments or stakeholders or externally to other members of the customer's sphere of influence.

This suggestion will likely be easier to implement with the full cooperation of marketing and service teams, but even lacking that support, it's critical that you add it to your standard approach.

Continue to Educate After the Sale

Providing customer training and support takes work, but it's also quite important. Some organizations view it as a necessary evil, while other, more innovative companies view it as a way to differentiate, upsell, and create additional profits.

The key to creating support that generates profit is to create support that's worth paying for. The way to do this is to make support a formal package. Think about it as a product and offer it either as a tangible added value or as an à la carte offering.

The Apple Genius Bar is a great example of a way to generate profits from support. Through its support system, Apple sells service packages, offers training programs, and even offers to recycle old products when you upgrade.

The question is, how can an individual salesperson learn from this approach and create more value by way of education after the sale?

Below are just five examples of how to turn your extraordinary service after the sale into a value, and perhaps into a revenue stream.

Live Q&A chats: When someone buys a product or service of any kind, you can offer reassurance that he will receive full value from his purchase by implementing regularly scheduled chat sessions where users or customers can ask questions about their purchase and receive help with features or implementations. This is also something you could offer as a presale education tactic as well as a paid subscription add-on.

There are many tools available that make this tactic fairly easy to implement. If you are a 37Signals software user, you probably already use its integrated chat tool, Campfire. There are other tools, such as Chatroll, that allow you to embed a group chat tool on your website for a simple branded option.

Drop-in Fridays: If your customers are primarily local, you may want to schedule a time when customers can come into your offices to receive additional advice or specific training, or to network with other users. They could even bring a product in with them.

Trade-in days: If you sell a product (such as technology) that is upgraded frequently or that forces you to go head to head with competitors, create and promote specific times when customers or prospects can come in and get credit for recycling an old version or upgrading to your product over a competitor's. Be prepared to offer a service that makes it both very attractive and very easy to switch.

This tactic lends itself to hard goods, but certainly software and other process-driven services could benefit from this approach as well.

Weekly Hangouts: As I've mentioned a number of times, one of my favorite tools is Google+ Hangouts. Using this tool, you can easily create video Q&A chats, offer weekly lessons, or simply create a series of expert adviser knowledge-sharing sessions to benefit your clients.

Online courses: Once someone buys a product or engages you to provide a service, you can easily establish a relationship of ongoing support through online courses.

The technology to create, manage, and deliver content using membership-site-building tools such as Kajabi or WordPress plug-ins like Wishlist Member makes this approach something that every business should consider as a way to expand offerings and generate a residual stream of revenue.

Creating even greater levels of support, delivering it in new and exciting ways, and making it worth paying for is how you make your level of service and authority stand out.

Don't Let the Transaction Kill Your Referrals

In far too many sales situations, once the sale is made, the salesperson disengages from the process. Add to that the fact that it's equally likely that the person who made the buyer decision in the first place isn't the one who will work with your organization on an ongoing basis, and you've got a clear recipe for miscommunication.

No matter how your organization chooses to move forward with a client once the contract is signed, you should plan to stay on top of how smoothly the "actual" process plays out to make sure that the transaction and start-up phases don't undo your great work.

One way superstar sales professionals adopt this kind of thinking is by considering themselves customer advocates. In other words, part of your job is to go to bat for what you promised your customer, particularly when she meets unintended resistance or confusion.

Below are several steps to consider as you build a *customer advocate system* that will turn the process of buying products and services into a personal brand- and value-building asset.

Remove all friction: Because we sometimes overautomate the sales process, we may end up making our customers do things that don't make sense to them. I'm all for automation, but we need to consider how it affects the customer experience and not always how it affects our workflow. Convenience is a tremendous relationship builder and differentiator. Look to add technology that works every time, doesn't require needless steps, and treats a customer like a human being, not a robot. Sure, this kind of stuff takes more time and effort, but it takes your competitors more time and effort too.

Overorient: The company autoresponder acknowledgement message won't cut it. Create an entire process in which you orient your customers to every aspect of your business, their transaction, expectations, and next steps. Build a new-customer kit and make this form of education an integral part of bringing your customers on for the long haul.

Surprise them: Overdeliver and surprise your new customers with something they didn't expect. This could take the form of additional training, additional services they didn't expect to receive, or simply a genuine gift of thanks. The key here is that you are delivering more than they expected. People love good surprises and few things get people talking faster than getting something they didn't expect. Lots of people get this idea, but remember your longtime customers too; sometimes in the rush to get new customers we forget about the ones who got us here.

Show gratitude: My mom taught me the importance of showing gratitude—and it's still great advice! You know you are thankful for the fact that people put down their hard-earned money for your product or service, but in the rush of business it can be easy to let the acknowledgement slip. Build gratitude into your process. Send handwritten notes every Friday, buy products from your customers and strategic partner (and send them as thank-yous), and pick up the phone and simply call to say thanks. Make saying "thank you" a habit. You'll get as much out of doing this as the person receiving your gratitude.

Referrals Take Education

Everyone wants referrals, but what we really want are referrals and introductions that fit—that match what we consider our ideal-client profile.

Our customers often are equally enthusiastic about providing referrals, but when we don't help them understand how to do this in the best possible way, we make their job that much more difficult.

Educating all of your referral sources, be they clients or strategic partners, helps guide the referrals process for the best possible results.

Your referral sources need to know the following five things.

1. *How would they spot your ideal client?* Describe your ideal client in such detail that most would have a hard time not identifying at least a handful of people who fit the model perfectly. Or better still, identify several actual prospective individuals or companies to use as examples. The more detail, including the types of challenges your ideal client might be facing, the better prepared your referral sources will be to make the right introductions.

2. *How would they best describe why they should work with you?* Hopefully you have a very clear understanding of this first. I often refer to this as your value proposition, or "why choose us?" Give your

referral sources the actual words to use to describe how you are different from everyone else that says they do what you do.

3. *What are some common trigger phrases they should listen for?* Whether you sell siding or software, people probably don't sit around with friends and discuss how they long for siding or software; usually, people talk about the problems in their lives. So, someone might say, "I sure hate painting my house every other year" or "My accountant is all over me because we can't ever produce accurate sales reports." These are what I call trigger phrases, and you should provide a solid list of the things hot prospects might actually say—a remark that shows they need something you offer— to your sources.

4. *What does your follow-up process entail?* Go ahead and tell your sources exactly how you intend to follow up with the referral and introductions you receive from them and exactly how you would like them to be involved. This helps turn a lead into an introduction and sets their minds at ease because you have a professional and valuable follow-up process rather than a hunt and kill approach.

5. *What's in it for them?* This last one may take many forms, but only in rare instances would I suggest offering some form of monetary incentive for referrals. It is a good idea, however, to reinforce two things—why this is a valuable thing for customers to do, and how much you appreciate it. Often, connecting referral generation with nonprofit support or allowing them to win something related to your business makes a lot of sense and can add some fun to the process.

You can create a one-page document, Web page, or just informally address each point in a meeting, but the key is to make it easy for your referral sources to do what they quite naturally want to do.

By systematically creating and running your own set of processes that apply after the sale, you automatically commit your sales activity to a much deeper level in a way that naturally adds value.

Allow Your Customers to Compete

Management consultant and author Peter Drucker famously coined the phrase "What gets measured gets done." While I agree with this completely, I would offer an enhancement: what gets measured gets done, but what gets measured and reported gets done exponentially.

Let me ask you this: Are your clients getting the absolute greatest results possible? Sure, a lot of that depends on their actions, but what could *you* do to get them to take greater action? What if you invoked some tried-and-true aspect of game mechanics to help your clients achieve greater results?

You're probably somewhat familiar with the concept. A weight-loss guru holds a competition to find the person who can lose the most weight; in the process, hundreds of her clients achieve far greater results due to the competition and the requirement to report their progress.

When clients have an incentive to report the progress they've made by following your program or using your product, they participate far more actively and experience far greater results. How could you get your clients to compete with one another for their own benefit?

The measured and reported model presents a profound opportunity for just about any type of business. The trick is to focus on the actions you know will allow your customers to get better results.

Perhaps it's making a game out completing training videos, creating a contest for returning required documents on time, or setting up a way to measure their progress using your product against the progress of all other product users. The MapMyRun tool does this for the runners' community; participants make it a game to measure and track fitness, but also to report progress to friends and other community members.

Here's a starter question to engage your own community this way: Can you find a reason to bring your customers together in a way that incentivizes them to measure and report the results they are getting with your products or services?

How about this? Let's say a group of business owners joins your eight-week coaching program. They are first asked to set goals; then over the next week they're measured and graded on the progress they make pursuing their goals. At the end of the program, the participant who makes the greatest progress receives a refund on the program.

One of the simplest ways to get started is to pool a number of clients and get them to compete based on results or progress. Offer a refund or prize for the person or company that records the greatest progress.

Similarly, you can use this approach to create a competition based on the number of referrals your client can generate for you.

Of course, if you have the right kind of business and a little creativity, you can hold a competition simply as a way to stimulate product sales. Buy X product during the month and tell us what it's done for you and we'll pick one winner each month to win Y.

The community-building aspects of this idea are intriguing as well. You could start a Facebook group based on your competition and watch your customers begin encouraging, aiding, and supporting one another in pursuit of their measured and reported progress.

I think this is one of the missing ingredients in so many businesses. No matter how great your training, consulting, or product, if you can't get people to do what's in their best interest, you can't help them achieve a result.

Anything you can do to help your clients get actual results will benefit your business in incredible ways. When your clients measure, report, and achieve greater results, they'll talk about you and the results you helped them gain.

Sometimes in the service of a client you must do everything you can to cajole, trick, or otherwise coax them into getting a result. And few things get people to take action like the accountability of competition.

Look at Where We've Been

By reading to this point in the book, you should now be well versed in the operation of the Sales Hourglass, and should have a very full understanding not only of the new sales mind-set, but also all the tools, techniques, and processes needed to start selling like a superstar.

You should also understand that the old ABC of sales—"always be closing"—is a thing of the past and that sales today is about connecting—leading the client on a journey that ends in his seeing results. In order to excel in this new context of selling, you must use everything you've learned—listening skills, content creation, your expert platform, your authority—to be the sales guide your clients want and need.

It is no longer appropriate to view prospects simply as prospects; you must view them as future advocates and referral sources.

If you're a salesperson on your own, you now have the information and insight to go off and think like a marketer while selling like a superstar.

The next section lays out a plan for those who need to pass these lessons on to others. If you manage sales teams, this will be invaluable for you. It can also be very valuable for those not in management, as a way to keep on track, share your learning with colleagues, or even teach your boss about the new sales world.

If you want to teach others how to thrive in the new world of sales, read on!

PART III

THE WORLD OF THE NEW SALES COACH

n parts I and II, I focused on the job of the individual salesperson. Individuals sellers, however, aren't the only ones who must adapt to the new world of sales. The job of the sales manager, VP of sales, sales trainer, and even of leadership and executive coaches has changed as well.

If we're now thinking of a sales professional as a sales guide, then the sales manager becomes something much more like a sales coach. Like any good coach, sales coaches need a game plan that addresses their current culture and helps steer the business away from traditional sales strategies and tactics.

If your organization is to have any chance of bringing sales and marketing to the same page, where collaboration and engagement are both understood to affect the buying process, you've got to take on the sales-coach mentality.

It doesn't matter if you're the owner of a company or the VP of sales. If you want to get the most from the model of a sales guide, it's essential to build a culture that makes it safe and productive for every member of your sales team to practice marketing-related tactics to meet sales objectives.

If you are responsible for managing, leading, or teaching a sales team, you might have skipped ahead to this section in order to get the material that seemed immediately relevant to your position. If so, I suggest you take the time to read the book from the beginning in order to get the full picture of the radical changes I've suggested.

If a member of your sales team suggested you read this book, there's a pretty good chance he or she is asking you to lead them through today's evolving world of sales.

Your role is as crucial as any in moving your team or company into the new sales world successfully. The following chapters cover the critical practices of the new sales coach.

CHAPTER 13

Change the Channel

The first order of business for the new sales coach is to take an assessment of how the sales channel integrates with the marketing channel. For some this might be a bit like asking you to acknowledge how well the two get along.

If you have a sales process, how was it built? How much input did your sales team have in creating the process, in determining compensation, and in figuring out what an ideal lead looks like?

If you are going to lead your current sales team into the world of inbound selling, social media, and reputation management, you'll likely need to tear some practices down, build new ones up, and make sure everyone realizes they are going to experience freedom, expectations, accountability, responsibility, and the function of sales in a totally new way.

So, let's start by addressing the elephant in the living room.

Has the world of inbound marketing made the salesperson unnecessary?

One answer is: it depends. The Internet has certainly turned the traditional act of selling solutions into a commodity act. There was a time when a salesperson's job was to find out what the prospect lacked and provide solutions, or at least information that led to a solution. But the Internet changed that job dramatically.

If you're still trying to push your sales team to sell solutions to a customer who has access to every possible bit of data—and the ability to create his or her own solutions based on these reams of virtual information—you're essentially doomed to selling on price or, worse, providing a negotiating chip to acquire the lowest price. In other words, you've turned your salespeople into a commodity.

If, however, you've come to realize that the salesperson's job is to find and create opportunities, change how people view what they might buy from your organization, and teach and facilitate discussions of industry trends and challenges, the answer to the question posed above is most definitely no.

My take on the difference between sales and marketing has always been that marketing's job was to own the message and the job of the sales professional was to own the relationship.

The meaning and delivery of the message, however, has changed. Marketers no longer have control over how the message is packaged and consumed.

Likewise, the meaning of "relationship" has changed. Salespeople have an entirely new set of tools to mine, build, nurture, and convert leads. Their success is no longer tied to relationships built on location.

In many ways, a salesperson's view could be that sales is the new marketing and marketing is the new sales support.

Salespeople who understand this can control their own destiny while delivering superstar results for any company and creating more value for any customer. Sales managers who get this can lead their teams to places where competitors don't even know to go.

Some of the new responsibilities a sales coach must embrace include teaching, leading, and empowering their teams.

A great deal of the work of leading a sales team today consists of helping them significantly shift how they view their work. Your responsibilities will include teaching salespeople how to create their own ideal-customer opportunities, coaching them in ways to differentiate themselves individually while upending the buying process, and bringing in new ways of thinking about typical customer challenges.

It will include teaching salespeople to think about and create educational content finely tuned and personalized for real customers.

It will be asking them to facilitate and lead community and peer-to-peer discussions and presentations between customers and strategic partners.

This dramatic change in the role of the effective salesperson won't be embraced by all for many years, which makes this precisely the right time for sales managers to embrace this new way of thinking and lead their teams out of the commodity business.

If the idea of empowering your sales team members to build their own expertise and authority makes you fear that they will simply grow into new roles and then leave, consider this: if you don't teach them the strategies and tactics contained in this book they will simply remain ineffective.

Would you rather build a reputation for creating superstars in your organization, even if that means some eventually go on to new opportunities, or manage mediocrity day in and day out?

Effective Sales Management Is both Integrated and Distinct

Over the years, the greatest breakdowns in many of the businesses that I've worked with lie in the divide between marketing and sales.

It might be tempting to conclude that what I'm referring to is a lack of sales, but what I'm really getting at is a misunderstanding of the distinction between sales and marketing.

Some of this might simply be semantics because the terms are used loosely and in varied ways, but here's what I find to be true: businesses either fail to address the sales and marketing functions as separate entities or choose to view selling as marketing. Either way, they end up limiting the effectiveness of both.

The trouble with this mind-set is that social media and inbound marketing have made the distinction even harder to appreciate. There was a time when marketing created brochures and salespeople delivered them. Today, prospects can create their own brochure of sorts using reviews, search engines, and social connections to find out about your company. They certainly don't need a salesperson to provide an information dump.

In the most traditional view, marketing is charged with lead generation, lead conversion, and customer experience. Lead conversion, or what one might think of simply as sales, is a central and separate function that must be wholly integrated into the entire marketing framework.

The tricky part is holding the terms "separate" and "integrated" in mind simultaneously.

Very often, lead generation dominates the marketing mind-set and sales is either not addressed in any systematic manner or it's simply left to "the sales guys" to do what they do. (Let's not even bring up how little thought is given to the customer experience part of marketing in this view.)

So it's no surprise that the greatest challenge most organizations face is getting sales and marketing on the same page.

Lead the Change Internally

The first step in building the sales department of the future is for those charged with leading the sales team to lead a much bigger change internally, one where the sales team members think like marketers but take their core skills out into the world of the individual customer. One where the marketing department no longer ignores or is threatened by requests from the field, but sees them as extremely important steps in the process of winning.

Below are recommendations for the sales manager who is willing to change the context of sales in the organization by demonstrating how to treat sales as a function of marketing while giving it the appropriate separation it deserves.

Bring your sales teams into marketing's planning phase: Field salespeople often understand the needs, wants, stories, and personas of an organization's best customers better than anyone else—yet they are rarely included in discussions about ideal clients and value propositions. Everyone involved in the marketing function (yes, this includes sales and customer-service people) should play a role in researching, crafting the message, outlining objectives, and determining how the marketing game is played from quarter to quarter.

Create an integrated sales process: If you follow the first suggestion, then it makes sense for the entire marketing department to play a role crafting an integrated sales process, not just the sales manager. Everyone involved in the selling function should have a clear process for discovery, presentation, nurturing, and converting. The process must be fully understood and supported by marketing and everyone must be taught how to conduct the process. One good way to start this process is to look to the most successful salespeople in the organization. Odds are they have your process up and running—ready to be mimicked.

Hire more educators and engineers: The common belief is that good salespeople are good relationship builders. While relationship building is crucial, it's often viewed in the light of outward social skills. In sales today, relationships are often judged not by the merits of likability, but by the merits of value. Prospects need a salesperson who can get them to think differently about a problem or teach them how to do something they don't yet understand. Your tech people might actually be the best people for this type of selling.

View sales as an extension of lead generation: As parts I and II attest, salespeople need to write and speak, just as they need to network and follow up. Smart salespeople understand that they are also in the business of brand building, reputation monitoring, and community management. Marketing departments and sales managers need to enable salespeople to produce content, participate in social networks, contribute expert articles, and get to podiums as often as possible.

Blur the lines between lead conversion and customer experience: I've said repeatedly that a sale isn't a sale until the customer receives the result he or she is expecting. This mind-set suggests that the sales staff should be intimately involved in measuring results, introducing new ways to use old products, solving problems, and digging up referrals at significant moments of truth.

The job of the new sales manager is to help the entire organization think differently about the role of sales, thereby effectively changing the sales channel.

CHAPTER 14

Swallow the Whistle

The sales coach has to teach the system, but he or she also has to adapt the system to the special needs of each team player.

A good coach cements the mind-set of the organization, protects the culture, and teaches critical thinking skills. To do this it's imperative that you build a systematic way to assess progress based on team members' unique abilities and provide coaching based on improving their strengths instead of meeting cold-call quotas.

I recommend creating an eight-week training program that teaches each sales guide how to listen online, identify ideal prospects, create warm leads, find problems, build a content platform, get to a podium, and increase his or her influence and authority in the market.

Just as important, if you want to make things happen and really change your sales game, you have to build your team up.

In his book *Taking People With You*, David Novak, CEO and chairman of Yum! Brands (KFC, Taco Bell, and Pizza Hut) recounts a story involving University of Kentucky basketball coach John Calipari. In 2009, Kentucky freshman John Wall was receiving loads of national attention as one of the best players in the game that year. Calipari noticed that team chemistry was starting to break down due to all the attention Wall was receiving.

Instead of ignoring this growing divide, Calipari pulled Wall aside and told him, "John, you are definitely the star of this team and you are definitely going pro. I want you to take as many of your teammates as you can with you. You need to make them great too."

That year Wall was indeed the number one pick in the pro draft, but four of his teammates also went in the first round—a feat that has never before been accomplished in college basketball.

Every team has superstars. Heck, maybe that's what got you promoted to managing the team in the first place. As a sales coach, though, your job is to take the entire team with you on a journey to success.

Coaching Is the New Managing

I believe that the role of the successful sales manager is strongly aligned with the role of a successful coach. This has probably always been true. A good manager helps employees succeed by helping them get better individually rather than getting them to adhere to a set performance standard. A good coach discovers the best way to put the parts together for the benefit of the team and then works to make the individual parts stronger.

While every generation develops its own view of work, the coaching model is particularly relevant for individuals identified as millennials, those born after about 1980.

The days of top-down, dictatorial management are quickly giving way to models that depend on collaboration, coaching, and the values of purpose, play, and passion.

The coaching model comes with specific practices that involve one-on-one give and take from both the coach and the team member. If sales managers are not chosen and groomed with this coaching model in mind, they may struggle with the practical realities of delivering this style of management.

The same holds true for individual salespeople. They, too, must be willing to accept the coaching approach that asks them to contribute, collaborate, and grow.

One of the things I've learned about the coaching relationship over the years is that it takes a certain kind of approach to get results—and if any kind of progress is to be made, a great amount of commitment is required of the person being coached.

Working with a coach in this arena revealed to me what I have come to believe are the most important attributes of the best coaching relationships.

Sales managers and sales professionals alike must understand and operate using the five principles that form the foundation of the coaching approach:

1. *Accountability*: Accountability is the easy one. If you know you should be improving your sales numbers and you have a meeting with your sales coach scheduled, you're probably going to practice and prepare more.

    But making people show up is only half of the accountability element. The real task is helping them determine what, based on their unique talents, they should be trying to achieve, and holding them accountable for making progress toward their stated objectives.

    A good coach will always spend a lot of time helping team members they mentor figure out specifically why they should set certain goals rather than telling them what the goals should be.

2. *Methodology*: I want any coach I work with to have a set point of view about what I'm trying to do and a proven, practiced, and repeatable process. That's not to say that I'm looking for cookie-cutter solutions, but you need to be able to spot patterns and mold experiences to a mentee's unique situation so that the practices are repeatable. It's the only way to truly measure progress and it's the best way to create momentum.

    Teach your process as part of your initial training with any salesperson.

3. *Behavior change*: The job that a coach performs—know it or not, admit it or not—is to change people's behavior. It's the only way that growth happens, habits get broken (and formed), and your people learn to attack any problem from a fresh framework. If you've ever tried to break a bad habit, you know that you can't simply use more willpower to overcome it. You have to change the underlying behavior—and perhaps the underlying reward for misbehavior—before anything happens.

    Maybe you've also succeeded in this category and seen for yourself the role that your beliefs played in your behavior change. If you don't coach people to change their habits, behavior, and beliefs as part of the entire plan, no matter what you hope to get your team members to do, you'll always come up short.

4. *Efficiency:* Here's an element that more coaches need to understand and use to their benefit. A really good coach will make employees better, faster. When you consider what your time is worth and multiply that by the gains achieved by helping your people reach their objectives, you can easily justify the extra personal attention you give to each person you coach.

5. *Measurement:* The only way to help your team members reach a goal or stay on track is to measure their progress. Most coaches know this and do this, and it's an absolute must.

   Resist the temptation to use measurement as another way to enforce quotas. You and your salesperson can define and measure anything you wish. What if you viewed this as your greatest tool for handing out recognition instead of a way of setting extreme goals?

   Change what you measure, and start small. Maybe your first job in getting a sales department turned around is to start recognizing people who show up every day with the right attitude. Sometimes that's the first step toward changing behavior.

   A good coach must help team members measure their progress in multiple ways and require them to report their progress and continually revisit their commitments.

Be the Change

So far this section has asked a lot of you. The truth is that the real opportunity to make change in your organization comes when you view your role as that of sales leader.

A great deal of what I've presented in this book pushes the view of the traditional sales professional far beyond where many are ready to go. My guess is that, in order to bring real change, that same shift will need to occur at every level of an organization.

I believe that as a new sales leader you must lead this change by thinking like an owner or an entrepreneur. You may not be an owner in the true sense, but your job and that of your sales team will be easier if you come to work with that mind-set every day.

An effective entrepreneur constantly seeks growth, paints a sharp vision for the team to follow, creates a culture of alignment, and leads by example—building a culture where everyone knows how to win.

In many ways, these are the tasks of the new sales coach and leader:

Work on you first—I've learned a great deal about leadership in the process of trying to build a business.

In sales, we often look to the most obvious areas for paths to growth, such as number of calls made, number of presentations made, or even improving someone's negotiating skills. The thing is, nothing really happens without true leadership.

That's not to say someone can't hatch a great sales process, get people to work their tails off, and grow a business that looks pretty successful. But without vision, compassion, purpose, and commitment, it's pretty hard to build a team environment in which people want to be their best selves. Getting a team to come to work as prepared and enthusiastic as possible may actually be the hallmark of a successful leader.

I'm like a lot of entrepreneurs: I want to work on the stuff the business makes and sells today. But leadership is quite often more about the stuff of tomorrow. It's messy and unruly and it gets in the way of things we'd rather do today.

And it takes work. It doesn't always come naturally to us, even those of us who are routinely thrust into roles that require us to lead in order for others to succeed. If you want to build a truly magical sales team, you've got to go to work on building your own leadership skills.

Grow yourself—Leadership is mostly about helping people grow and realize their full potential. Of course, the only way you can provide an environment where this can happen is by charging headlong down that path yourself. Unless you are constantly experiencing your own growth, you'll cease to recognize the need for it in others.

Reading is probably my most effective tool for growth. I read everything I can find that's related to my work, but I make it a point to read a great deal of fiction, as well as books on other, seemingly unrelated topics such as spirituality, psychology, sociology, nature, ancient religious traditions, and even architecture. I'm fascinated by the connections these subjects make to things like community building and system development.

Start asking for recommendations on books about leadership. Don't be surprised if a few of them don't have the word "leader" in the title.

Create vision—People don't give themselves to great companies or great products. They follow great stories and great causes and great ideas. Until your leadership ideas are steeped in a vision that's bigger than simply meeting this month's sales quota, you'll struggle to attract anyone interested in much more than that. Vision takes thinking bigger for yourself and your entire team first. Until you can do that, you'll find it hard to inspire yourself, let alone those who might choose to join you.

Do you have a big idea? Are you headed somewhere really cool? Do you work with a higher purpose in mind? Share that with your team. Don't be afraid to inspire others to think bigger in the process—that's vision.

To get started, ask yourself this question: What's your picture of your business in three years and why is that a vision worth following?

Get alignment—Get people involved in developing the sales journey by making them understand why they are doing what they do. Ask for their input and ideas and then hold them accountable for improvement based on their input. Give them permission to disagree with you—even invite conflict. Ask that surprises and bad news be delivered unvarnished. It's the only way to get people as invested as you are in the outcome of their work and it's a way you'll eventually get everyone aligned.

Bring your entire sales team together and ask them to identify, in their view, the three greatest priorities in your department right now. Then develop an attack plan for those three priorities and start working immediately on accountability checkpoints.

Teach by example—This one is obvious, but so hard to do consistently. If you sit around and complain about those darn customers, don't be surprised if everyone else does too. If you want people to be on time for meetings, show them how important it is by arriving ten minutes early and then starting on time. If you want your staff to go overboard showing clients their appreciation, demonstrate that behavior by sending handwritten notes to clients each week.

Identify three behaviors that you want everyone to model and make it your place to lead them there by example.

Build a culture of winning—It's disheartening to see organizations where managers manage by monopolizing control and making sure that everyone has to come to them for answers. Perhaps the most universal truth about leadership is that the best way to succeed as a leader is to put all of your energy into helping those you lead succeed. In *Good to Great,* Jim Collins notes that many of the best leaders built such a strong culture of winning that their departments learned to manage without them.

Ask yourself what would fall apart in your team if you needed to leave for a few months. Go to work on building leadership in those areas by empowering other members of your team to learn and teach the most important skills every team member must master.

Believe in people—I've found that people pretty much live up to our expectations. While it's pretty easy to take credit when people succeed and place blame when they don't, most of the time it comes down to what we expect. Expect more of people and they'll rise to the occasion. Believe in people; they'll do more than we expect—and get more involved in the success of the company.

Give each member of your team a thirty-minute one-on-one meeting each week for which they get to set the agenda. Ask them to think about what they need to be successful and engaged and assure them you want to go to work on that with them.

This leadership stuff isn't that complicated; it just takes work. Make leadership creation a priority and build it into the culture of how your business functions. If your vision of success involves anything more than what you can wrap your arms around today, you need to understand how to become a better leader.

Closely measure what you can control—In a recent study, the Sales Education Foundation and Vantage Point Performance identified 306 metrics that sales leaders used to manage their businesses. As is the case in most organizations, a great deal of what people measured fell into two categories that were largely out of their control—sales objectives (things like new customers, repeat sales, and retention) and business objectives (things like profit, growth, and customer satisfaction).

The remainder of the metrics fell into the category of sales activities, things like number of accounts per rep, opportunities created, account management, and territory management. While a great deal of time was spent on things like sales forecasts, the truly effective sales manager spent time on managing sales activities such as teaching salespeople to better identify ideal prospects, building authority, and discovering ways to go deeper into understanding the needs and opportunities in existing accounts.

Habits of Sales Leaders

It's pretty easy for salespeople to let themselves get buried behind a computer screen and forget that the world out there is an amazing place to turn up new opportunities.

Sure, you want them taking care of customers, writing sales letters, and growing their referral base, but in order for salespeople to truly evolve, sometimes you have to help them evolve their environment.

Many fish can grow only to a size that matches the size of their environment. Put a fish in a small tank and it stays small; put a fish in a big tank and it can grow bigger. I believe this metaphor applies to how humans adapt to the work environment as well.

One of the surest ways to grow your team's sales muscle, to help them become leaders in their chosen marketplace, is to go to work on getting them to better their industry. One of your jobs is to help your team become market leaders.

You can apply this thinking locally, in your marketplace, or globally, depending upon where you start, but organizations that embrace this way of thinking generally show up as leaders in every category of business.

Below are a handful of habits that market leaders embrace, habits that you must encourage your sales teams to develop.

Network: Market leaders understand that networking is a way of life, not just a lead-generation practice. Networking is how you uncover opportunities, solutions, employees, mentors, and referrals and it's how you and your team build best-of-class resources to bring value to every aspect of your life and that of your customers.

Networking involves giving and receiving but does not involve scorekeeping. The first reflex in market leader networking should be, "Whom can I help?"

Participate: Nearly every industry has an association or group on the local, national, or international level whose purpose is to improve, protect, and grow the interests of the industry or community.

One of the things I've learned over the years is that market leaders participate in such groups. They join them, attend events, and volunteer to serve on boards and committees. This is such a strong trait of a market leader that I've long used it as a defining element to help describe what, for my organization, makes an ideal client. If you sell in a B2B world, targeting individuals who participate at a high level in their industry groups is a smart play.

Teach: Successful businesses have usually figured something out that others have not. Market leaders have figured something out that others have not and they teach it. They facilitate discussions with their peers, conduct workshops on various best practices related (and unrelated) to their core business, and view their internal culture much more as a school than a workplace.

Cooperate: Here's where I may get some pushback, but in my experience, market leaders view competition differently than others. Market leaders believe that cooperation is far more fruitful than competition and look for ways to collaborate, educate, and even help industry members that some might view as direct competitors.

Now, you may draw the line at publicly sharing the secret sauce that makes your business profitable. Realize, however, that the world is a tremendously abundant place and cooperation is a much bigger long-term leadership strategy than competition.

Host: Finally, market leaders understand the value of playing the role of host for their community.

They invest in spaces that allow people to come together, whether there is a valid customer-generating case to be made or not. They host industry meetings and events. They look for ways to gather two or more people together to have lunch—or to celebrate music, art, or education.

Leadership isn't really about being better or stronger or faster; it's more about your gut reaction to things around you and what you do about it. Taking action that benefits your industry, tribe, or community as a whole is how you establish a market leader mind-set.

CHAPTER 15

Bridge the Gap

As suggested in previous chapters, the new sales coach is a bridge builder, charged with closing the gap between the marketing and sales functions.

One of the best ways to do this is to get marketers and salespeople to understand and talk to each other. That may sound simplistic, but it's the way you do it that will make a difference.

If you were to take a truly customer-centric view of things today, you could say that everyone in the organization is in sales and everyone in the organization is in marketing. But how do you make that practical?

Sales, marketing, and support must get into one another's business. They should continue performing specific functions, while intentionally overlapping.

Forming Customer-centric Action Teams

As I've shown in this book, the most potent approach to marketing and sales involves blending inbound marketing with inbound selling.

The challenge in implementing such an approach lies squarely in an environment of intense cooperation between marketing and sales. As anyone in sales management can attest, reconciling the two isn't always an easy task.

But if marketing and sales adopt parallel inbound approaches without total harmony, they may actually increase the internal working gap and muddle the message ultimately heard by the market.

What if you led your organization in a direction that not only puts sales and marketing on the same team, but did so in a way that truly puts the customer first? What if, in place of giving lip service to this idea, as so many organizations do, you broke your marketing, sales, support, and service teams into small units and compelled them to work on individual client segments or specific accounts as self-managed action teams?

One potential way to set up such an arrangement would be to assign team leaders and rotate each member through the role of leader every sixty or ninety days. This would put accountability and autonomy directly on every member of the team. The result would be a shared result, owned by all, with no way to point fingers and pass blame on either marketing or sales.

If you use this approach, you might be quite amazed by the culture of collaboration that forms. Certainly, in your role of coach, you'll need to guide these teams in the most productive ways, but this is how you create the kind of communication that leads to real innovation. You just might find that this changes your entire business model.

To ease into such an arrangement, bring your sales team members into marketing meetings to share what they are hearing on the street. You might even go as far as requesting that the marketing department develop some questions to pose to clients and prospects as a way to collect meaningful data on the client's world.

The next logical step in integration is to ask members of the marketing, service, and support teams to participate in routine "ride alongs" with sales reps. That way, they can make calls on clients and prospects, engage in valuable conversations with them, and gain a better understanding the world of sales.

When you're getting sales and marketing on the same page, take care to inject a bit of empathy into the process. When team members gain a better understanding of one another's objectives and challenges, they are often better prepared to look for collaborative solutions to customer challenges.

This alone may turn up some customer-friendly processes and touchpoints, but to make this new learning pay off, you need to create cross-functional teams charged with blending inbound marketing and inbound selling.

Once your teams start blending objectives and collaborating on behalf of prospects and customers, it's time to go to work finding and documenting the best practices and successful processes the teams will inevitably develop. You can then use this approach to build a truly personalized, customer-oriented marketing and sales methodology.

Enter the Marketing Hourglass

In part I, I explained a concept I call the Marketing Hourglass. The Marketing Hourglass is a framework you can employ to define how your customer-centric teams might work together. You can use it to define roles, establish projects, and even create specific playbooks for customers, products, and services.

Think of the Marketing Hourglass as a series of stages that make up the customer life cycle, starting from the point at which a prospect comes to know about your business through the point at which she becomes a loyal referral champion.

Effective marketing is always about leading a customer on a journey through the stages that allow him or her to determine that your solution is the perfect solution at the perfect time. When a prospect is led on the journey properly, he or she comes to the decision to buy via a much more collaborative path.

When this is the case, effective marketing lessens the need for what many associate with the most negative aspects of selling—hard closing, arm-twisting, and constant pestering.

The shape of the Hourglass derives from the well-work funnel, but actually draws upon the notion that the job of marketing is much broader in the phases prior to and after a sale and only gets more narrowly focused during the try and buy phases required to make a sale.

More than ever before, the job of the superstar sales coach is to help the organization understand the integrated yet separate nature of the sales function.

Many organizations lack an effective Marketing Hourglass approach and consequently the field sales team is left to chase leads that may not have been properly attracted, educated, or defined.

The typical "lead scoring" approach tends to lean heavily on leads who raise their hands and volunteer to be sold to rather than on attracting ideal leads ready to go on a highly personalized journey.

This is where the superstar sales professional shines. Many salespeople understand that the most effective leads are quite often those they are able to identify and nurture long before any lead-scoring process can begin to identify them.

Don't get me wrong—marketing can be extremely important in terms of opening doors for sales teams, but effective sales coaches know that they must also teach a sales process that takes the best that marketing creates and personalizes and amplifies the value for the individual prospect on a case-by-case basis.

This is the place where marketing and sales—integration and independence—merge.

In chapter eleven, I detailed the Sales Hourglass. This process, built specifically for the sales function, takes its cue from the Marketing Hourglass and is deeply integrated into many of the phases of a healthy Marketing Hourglass. It's vital that a sales coach understands the framework and processes of both Hourglasses.

In a traditional Marketing Hourglass approach, it's quite likely that the middle of the Hourglass—the try and buy phases—is where the sales team would be asked to step in.

I believe that a much smarter sales process asks the sales team to get involved both earlier and later in the buying process so that they can personalize the journey *before, during* and *after* the sale.

One of the most important jobs of the new sales coach is to build, integrate, and train the sales team on the use of the Sales Hourglass approach to sales. Developing and teaching a sales process that is highly integrated with the marketing process while taking advantage of the sales team's unique ability to deliver value on the level of the individual prospect is the ultimate mission of today's sales coach.

Throughout this book I've suggested that sales reps who learn to think like marketers will make themselves far more valuable to their organization. The sales coach or manager who understands how to use his or her position to bring sales and marketing together may become the most sought-after manager in any organization.

The Sales Hourglass for the Sales Coach

As suggested above, the Sales Hourglass is a path a salesperson can take, in conjunction with the marketing process, to help a prospect become engaged in the specific process of buying.

As a sales coach you can think of the Sales Hourglass as the prospect tool that will help your sales team members tailor their sales approach to each client. One of the greatest benefits of a structured tool such as this one is that it keeps a salesperson focused on the next step, even if that next step is the decision to pursue other opportunities.

The Sales Hourglass is a client-focused approach designed to deliver the best possible result for the client while allowing the sales professional to more effectively land business. Because the process is so steeped in the client's most pressing needs, the act of documenting and sharing the Sales Hourglass process with a prospect may in itself allow your organization to stand out. It introduces useful steps not often taken by traditional sales professionals—steps that demonstrate not only a better way to sell, but also a better way to buy.

Another way of thinking about the Sales Hourglass is that it's the perfect tool to use to align your selling process with the prospect's buying process. When you do that, you not only sell more, you make the process of buying more valuable.

Or as Jill Rowley of Oracle puts it: "The modern sales professional is actually *not* a seller, but is someone who helps people buy. This is someone who helps the buyer understand her problem, helps the buyer understand there's a solution to the problem, and helps the buyer understand why her company is uniquely qualified to solve the buyer's problem."

The key difference between the two Hourglass applications is that while the Marketing Hourglass is broadly cast at an ideal-client persona or description, the Sales Hourglass is focused on an individual prospect or need and operated at a much more personal level.

Another core difference is that the journey through the Sales Hourglass must be based on the understanding that you and the buyer are prepared to determine that there may not be a journey at all.

In the traditional always-be-closing mind-set, salespeople were often encouraged to go for the order no matter what. This often resulted in customers being let down when it turned out the product wasn't a good fit or that their organization wasn't prepared for the solution the salesperson foisted upon them.

A sales superstar recognizes when a fit is not a fit and serves the client's long-term needs by helping them find the best fit—even if today that means sending them toward a competitor.

The Sales Hourglass Playbook

Playbooks are used in many business settings, but a more familiar definition may come from the world of sports. In football, for example, the coach will use a playbook to quickly assess a current situation, such as third down and long, and draw from a range of set plays.

The Sales Hourglass playbook aligns specific sales and marketing strategies and tactics with tools, content, and coaching that allows a sales rep to align his or her sales process with the prospect's buying process.

As a reminder, the stages of the Sales Hourglass are as follows:

Explore—The explore phase, as the name suggests, is the place where a sales professional might conduct his own research, such as exploring the elements of an organization's community, constructing stakeholder maps, and uncovering problems he can make visible.

Collaborate—The next step is to take what he's learned and assumed in the exploration state and start talking with a prospect about innovations.

Design—This step takes what he's learned while exploring and collaborating; he begins to design a solution with the customer and with the company.

Define—Once a salesperson has effectively crafted a solution with and for the prospect, he begins defining how the solution will be structured, delivered, implemented, and paid for.

Deliver—In many organizations, once a deal is inked, the salesperson's job is done. Customer service, project teams, or delivery experts take over. There are many good and practical reasons for this kind of handoff, but I believe the true expansion of your value comes from staying very active with the client after the sale.

Measure—Quite often the value of a solution can't be easily measured, and yet measurement is an essential element. The Sales

Hourglass performance operates at a much higher level when the sales team becomes obsessed with measuring, analyzing, and communicating the value their customers receive.

Engage—It's amazing how often sales professionals neglect to engage past customers until it's time to reorder or time to review a contract. Frequently reengaging customers through continued education and exploration is what leads to the discovery of new opportunities, new introductions, and referrals.

Let's outline some of the tools, content, and coaching that might go into a basic Sales Hourglass playbook.

Explore—Teach your team to identify ideal prospects and surround them socially. Be where they are, read what they read, and build a map of their connections. This is how you spot opportunities for connection and problem solving.

Collaborate—Take what you've learned in the exploration phase and start sharing relevant content with the prospect. Start building case studies and stories related to challenges your prospect may be facing.

Design—Once a prospect starts to respond to your personalized information sharing, you can begin to explore potential opportunities to design a solution to needs you helped her identify and perhaps think differently about.

Define—At this stage you'll need to give her a taste of how your proposed design might actually work. Below is an example of a tremendously effective way to approach this critical and often mishandled step.

An effective way to move from *define* to *deliver*

I've been selling a service for many, many years and I can tell you that selling people something they can't touch and feel has its challenges. No amount of explaining, documenting, and outlining can replicate the conditions of actually experiencing the service in action.

That's why I've always felt that the best way to effectively sell a service is to start by giving it away.

(cont'd on next page)

(cont'd from previous page)

Here's how that might play out in, say, a consulting model.

- A prospective client hears you present some valuable information in a webinar.
- Some of the things you touched on directly hit on an issue he's struggling with.
- He calls you up and asks you to come out and present some ideas on working those issues.
- Instead of agreeing to what is basically a sales call, you suggest another approach.
- You send him the detailed form you use in the discovery phase of working with a client and ask that each member of his executive team complete the form.
- When you meet, you simply begin consulting with them by conducting a session that helps the team get aligned on key issues, based on their form responses.
- At the end of the allotted time you make observations and a global recommendation to solve their issue.
- They determine they would like to see a proposal on how you could help them as a team.

The reason this approach is so effective is that no real selling has to happen. You get to control the course of the entire meeting, the client gets value whether he agrees to hire you or not, and you get a valuable start in the engagement, trust, and information aspects of the work should he agree to move forward.

This is exactly the approach I've used for a number of years. It always leads to a more productive sales call and it effectively allows the prospective client to experience just a bit of what it would be like to work with me.

Deliver—Once the contract is signed, in order for a long-term, referral relationship to exist, the sales professional must stay attuned to the ongoing needs of the client. Build a process wherein the sales professional can act as a client advocate and play a role in the smooth transition from buying process to customer experience.

Measure—In order for sales professionals to gain the greatest understanding of the value they're delivering to clients, it's important to implement a process that asks them to participate in results reviews with the clients. At a predetermined date they should initiate a process designed to determine the level of results achieved by their clients. This is the point in the relationship where testimonials, case studies, and referrals are developed.

Engage—The final step in all account management is measured engagement through continued education and ongoing assessment of further client needs. Again, this should become a predetermined process that is initiated by the sales professional managing the account.

As you develop your playbook, be sure to collaborate with your sales team to amplify their current best practices and most effective tools. Also make sure to include marketing in any discussion regarding current or future content needs. When you guide marketing assets in this fashion, you can often help them create much more useful content.

Your job as a sales coach is to teach your sales team to use these steps as a framework for developing individual-prospect playbooks—the tool that outlines their strategy for winning business with a client.

Start Bridging the Gap

By this point, I sincerely hope your mind is swimming with ideas for bridging the gaps between the marketing, sales, and service functions in your organization.

The small, elite, focused team approach that involves your marketing, sales, and service functions is the best framework for creating a team environment internally and the best way to serve the customer externally.

Start a discussion with your sales team around these seven questions and then take that discussion to every corner of the marketing function in your business.

1. How can you begin to involve your sales team members in the creation of content specifically tailored to customer needs?
2. How can you get your sales team members thinking about curating content with specific industries or clients in mind?
3. How can you get your sales team members involved in creating, collecting, and personalizing content from and with their customers?

4. How can you get your sales team members to focus on creating educational experiences worth paying for?
5. What could your sales team members do to make the experience of buying as remarkable as the lead-up to being sold?
6. What can your sales team members do to add and measure value as a way to stay top-of-mind with existing customers?
7. What can your sales team members do to plant the seed for referrals in the sales process and create opportunities to reward referral champions?

Now that you've moved to change the conversation between sales and marketing and hopefully moved sales, service, and marketing into a more integrated mind-set, it's time to build the ultimate sales tool—your unique sales methodology. This is the tool that will allow you to amplify everything we've built to this point and build a sales culture that will allow your sales team to stand out in the market.

CHAPTER 16

Find Your Method

As the coach of your sales team, you need your team to buy into your system. To help them do this, you've got to create a sales process or methodology that allows them to succeed while differentiating their efforts from the rest of the market.

Think of your sales group as a community. As I noted in chapter two, people don't join directives or training; they join methods, unique points of view, and processes surrounded with branding. To solidify this community, you must create a common language your team can share with one another and with customers. (As mentioned earlier, quite often your success model exists in the self-created process of one or two of your best salespeople.)

In part II, I outlined a sales process call the Sales Hourglass. This approach is steeped in today's need to make the sales experience as valuable as the products and services an organization offers.

The process makes heavy use of the fact that the sales team members need to become much more involved in tactics traditionally seen as the focus of marketing, including defining ideal clients, creating value proposition, building authority and expertise, and managing individual reputations.

In this chapter, we'll look at the elements you can use to design your unique process and sales methodology in the context of a sales manager's need to develop, document, and train a team to use this process.

Do You Have a Sales Process?

To begin with, you need to figure out if your department or those you are training even have a workable sales process. This isn't a judgment so much as an observation; some organizations just aren't that systems driven.

Most organizations have some sort of sales process either because the current salespeople figured out their own over time or because their organization trained them in a specific method for moving a lead from inquiry to close. In this regard, a sales process is really little more than a standardized set of steps that are turned into a process in order to create consistency.

Have you documented your standardized sales process? Could you, if asked, take someone through the process from start to finish?

The most common sales approach goes something like this: a prospect demonstrates interest, the salesperson digs for pain, presents a solution, handles objections, proposes a purchase, wrestles with terms, handles more objections, and goes in for the close.

Some firms have embraced a more so-called adaptive approach, one that zeroes in on understanding and controlling the buying process itself: how a buying decision is made, what selection criteria are used, how benefits are quantified, and, most important, how funding for the purchase is allocated.

While both of those approaches can and do work to some extent for many firms, I'd like to suggest another way—a way that moves your people out of the conversation that simply tries to win the fight for "why choose us?"

The problem with a sales process that attempts only to answer "why choose us over a competitor?" is that it keeps your sales team in the commodity race, where someone will always be able to change—and control—the game using price as a leading tool.

Why Choose Anything?

The best way to effectively eliminate competition is to own the question, "Why choose anything?" In other words, use the question in the sales process as a way to help prospects discover and solve problems they didn't realize existed.

This is how you add extreme value while building a reputation that makes your organization and sales team members welcome at any discussion.

My friend and coach extraordinaire, Dan Sullivan, founder of Strategic Coach, shared his definition of selling. I think it's a mind-set that accurately frames the objective of selling as described throughout this book: "Selling is getting someone intellectually engaged in a future result that is good for them and getting them to emotionally commit to take action to achieve that result." Salespeople who use this mind-set are able to build long-term value with their clients.

Teaching the "why choose anything?" mind-set involves three potent action steps:

1. *Making problems visible*: Salespeople who can help organizations uncover problems that are masked by unrelated symptoms hold a distinct competitive advantage. For example, companies often try to apply a new software or process to fix what's actually a culture issue. By embracing the community channel model described in chapter two, salespeople can clearly diagnose this paradox and not only point a prospect in a more profitable direction, but also help them better understand how this challenge may be at the root of other challenges.

2. *Making solutions easy*: One of the greatest challenges to successful engagements is acquiring the ability to make a proposed solution easy to understand, embrace, and implement. Ideas are a dime a dozen, but results come from successfully executing ideas. Today's best salespeople are able to propose elegant solutions that are easy to explain and measure. This ability comes from digging into the DNA of an organization to understand how to approach solutions as collaborative efforts.

3. *Using teaching to sell*: In chapters ten and eleven, I outlined the very specific approach a salesperson today must take to build authority through the process of educating through content (written and spoken). The consistent application of these tactics positions salespeople as teachers and experts and effectively changes how a prospect views the value salespeople can provide. Prospective clients need salespeople to provide insight over information and will no

longer tolerate a sales experience that does not employ the teaching model.

The Secret to Owning Insight

The greatest way to deliver value to a prospect or customer is through insight—helping her understand her business challenges in ways that were previously a mystery to her.

In chapter two, I introduced a process I call deconstructing community. This is a process which, when completed by individual salespeople, allows them to uncover and make problems visible in ways that other salespeople won't even consider.

In order to bring insight and stand out with prospects, you've got to know more about their business than they do. You've got to be able to teach them how to think about their business and show them what they need, even though they may have no idea they need it. Teaching salespeople how to properly dig into community is how you enable them to access this deeper knowledge.

Reprentatives from a large software company came to us with a familiar challenge. They were growing steadily and were quite profitable, but they couldn't attain the kind of growth they thought they should.

They had a very sharp focus and were quite clear about how their solution was different from their competitors'. They had little trouble explaining their unique approach and their clients seemed quite happy. Their staff often talked about how they felt they weren't just providing a software solution, they were changing an industry for the good. And yet, they didn't get as many opportunities to tell their story as they would have liked.

When we reviewed their business, it was clear that the marketing focus they had adopted was simply a sales process. The sales process was very good and very effective, but where they were lacking was in being found. In other words, when prospects went looking for a solution, our client's point of difference wasn't being found.

They had a great sales process, a great service process, and a great product, but had little in terms of demonstrated thought leadership and audience development.

By looking closely at the content they were producing on a consistent basis and where they were engaging potential clients, it became clear that there were some major holes in their community.

They had a grand story to tell, but it wasn't being told and shared in the right places. We also discovered that they had totally neglected building community around the end users of their software—their clients' clients—and this gap offered a vivid opportunity to address their growth goals.

Community forms around a business through the following six elements. The more you can teach salespeople to recognize and mine these elements, the more prepared they'll be to add value in the process of selling.

The first step in analyzing a prospect is to dig into each of these six channels and make some initial determinations about how they might affect your approach to working with a prospect or working more deeply with an existing customer.

Clarity action steps: Uncover a handful of customers and employees of the prospect you are targeting and plug them into a CRM tool like Nimble to monitor their public social media activity. It's amazing what you can learn about an organization by watching how they interact in places like Facebook and Twitter. If you can find a way to ask questions of a few of their staff members or customers, even better. You're looking for clues as to what the market really thinks of their brand. This is also a nice way to uncover some opportunities and unmet needs.

Culture action steps: If you have any luck uncovering an organization's employees, ask them what they think about working for their company. This can be a way to understand an organization more deeply than their website marketing-speak could ever reveal.

See if you can find examples of how the company culture sees itself, in elements like mission statements, core values, and the like. Based on the initial clarity step, do these seem to fall into line with some sort of higher purpose of why the organization exists? Can you think of a single word that the market might use to describe their brand?

Method action steps: Dig into companies' white papers, ebooks, and brochures. Do they seem to rally around a unique point of view or way of doing business? Do they use and promote their own terminology, processes, and checklists? By monitoring customers and mining social networks like Twitter you may discover they have created a community of customers who are able to speak to one another using a common language.

Content action steps: Start to build a library of every bit of content the organization puts out. You can learn a great deal about what they value and perhaps where gaps exist by understanding an organization's approach to creating content. Here you're looking for ways that distinguish how they use content to communicate what's important. You're also looking for gaps—what content types seem to be missing altogether.

Is the company using content to build awareness, trust, and engagement or do they employ it only when they try to sell? Become a customer and see how they use content in the sales and follow-up process. What do their e-mail responses to inquiries look and sound like? Is their content intentionally sharable?

Presence action steps: Collect as much advertising, public relations, social network, and referral activity as you can. Subscribe to e-mail newsletters and campaigns. Engage in social media contests and "asks."

Is the company sending a clear and integrated message? Do elements occur that don't seem to go together? Does their marketing presence match the clarity and culture research you've done?

Touchpoint action steps: Your job is to construct a map, using the Hourglass concept, of all the ways you see an organization engaging prospects and customers. The simplest approach is to create a grid and then add ways that your prospect creates awareness and builds trust. Try to map out their sales and customer service processes. Again, see if there's a way you can become a customer or community member by purchasing, subscribing, and/or attending events whenever possible.

No matter what you sell, some of your greatest opportunities will come from understanding the gaps found in your research subject's marketing.

Merging the Sales and Marketing Hourglasses

In order for a sales process to be most effective, it must be designed and implemented in a way that fully integrates and supports the overall marketing efforts.

Even though you may design a sales system that opens doors and creates opportunities, without integrating sales and marketing you will find that later on in the sales process you may confuse your customers by sending messages and supporting positions that conflict with what the organization is saying and doing on its website or in social media through its marketing.

That's why I've spent so much time throughout this book talking about traditional marketing approaches such as the Marketing Hourglass. You can't support or supplement something you can't see or understand.

That's not to say that you, as a sales coach or trainer, don't understand marketing. My guess is that most sales managers actually understand many of the customer-facing elements of marketing better than a typical marketing MBA. It's just that you're not beating down the door and demanding a seat at the marketing table.

This goes the other way as well. One of your jobs as the sales leader is to demand that marketing become involved in your sales process, understand your Sales Hourglass, and integrate your findings with their strategy and positioning.

Once you build the Sales Hourglass that fits your specific selling objectives, start creating and documenting tools that can be used both as the starting point for training your sales team and as bridge-building tools to educate the marketing team. Use these tools as the basis for all of your internal departmental training and as a way to present the new context of sales to the entire organization.

As you can see, this approach goes much deeper into the function of selling than simply probing for solutions and fitting needs.

Defining a methodology such as this one is how you formally bring marketing and sales onto the same page. This is the real leadership opportunity this way of thinking presents.

Visualizing Your Stages in CRM Fashion

Once a combined sales and marketing initiative designs a way to move prospects and customers through your business, you can attach the Marketing Hourglass and Sales Hourglass labels to stages in your organization's CRM system. That way, you can keep tabs on the work you have left to do in your relationship-building system.

Once you define and label the logical path you're using to deepen your customer relationships, use your CRM tool to visualize where every lead and customer is located in your Sales Hourglass. This gives you the ability to easily view where the system is breaking down and where it's working well.

To further integrate sales into this intentionally staged approach, try to view each prospect in one stage (or phase) as a lead for the next phase. For example, a customer in the *design phase* should be looked at and treated as a new lead for the *define phase.* And once a customer moves to the *deliver phase,* for example, he or she is now a hot prospect for your measure campaign (but only then).

This mind-set allows you to build better processes, such as results reviews and additional educational touchpoints, both aimed at moving prospects to that next stage.

What I've suggested throughout this book is that the only way to get sales and marketing truly working together is to extend the participation of the sales team to every stage of the Marketing Hourglass and involve the marketing team in the various stages of the Sales Hourglass.

Only when you develop this common language can both teams better support and interact with each other's specific initiatives.

CHAPTER 17

Rethink Hiring

I f we accept the idea that the role of the salesperson and the various implications of strategic thinking, problem finding, and content creation that go with that role have changed, it can't be much of a stretch to suggest that the makeup of the prototypical star salesperson has changed as well.

Dexterity, empathy, pattern recognition, and a whole lot of technology wrangling should have organizations rethinking what a sales guide looks like. In *Re-imagine!*, Tom Peters famously suggested that companies should "hire freaks" and "fire all male salespeople" as a way of highlighting just how stuck in ruts he believes most companies are:

"Freaks keep us from falling into ruts. (If we listen to them.) (We seldom listen to them.) (Which is why most of us—and our organizations— are in ruts. Make that chasms.)"

My father was a salesman in the classic Willy Loman way, but without the tragedy. He got up every morning, packed his bags every week, and went on the road to exchange his time and information for the monetary reward of an order.

However, he knew, and stated often, that everyone sells for a living— he just happened to *know* that's what he did.

My friend and fellow author Dan Pink likes to say that "while not everyone seeks sales in the classic selling sense, we all seek resources other than money." Has that fundamentally changed the view of who and what makes a classic salesperson? I think it has.

When I write a blog post, I am selling. When I speak at a conference, when I talk to a journalist, when I refer another business—I'm selling. All of these activities collectively make up the world of sales today just as surely as an appointment for the stated purpose of getting someone to buy my wares.

Few people have addressed the changing manner in which the world of sales works over the past decade better than Dan Pink, author of *To Sell Is Human: The Surprising Truth About Moving Others.*

Pink's earlier books—*Drive, A Whole New Mind,* and *Free Agent Nation*—defined working trends that have become accepted norms in the world of work today. Prior to becoming a free agent in his own right, Pink wrote speeches for Vice President Al Gore and helped sell a nation on ideas worth investing in. His TED talk, "*The Puzzle of Motivation,*" has been viewed nearly five million times.

While the need to sell in any environment has perhaps become more important than ever, the role of the traditional salesperson has forever been altered in ways that require us to rethink what it even means to be a salesperson.

Traditionally, the stereotypical view of the salesperson was that of the outgoing go-getter who possessed secret information. Today's successful salesperson, as I've outlined in this book, must be an amalgam of marketer, educator, information seeker, and innovator.

According to Pink, this is not a change in degree, it's a fundamental change in kind.

The days of transactional selling are over. The days of solution selling are also coming to an end because today's primary sales skill is problem finding—correctly identifying and solving problems people don't even realize they have.

Because selling is problem finding *and* problem solving, the idea of selling now must be woven through everything that everyone in the organization is doing.

In *To Sell Is Human,* Pink cites an example of a company doing a quarter of a billion dollars in sales but claims they have no sales force. Their view is simple: they have no salespeople because everyone is a salesperson.

The implication of this idea is extremely important for both salespeople and those who need to hire, train, and retain salespeople in today's market.

Introducing the Ambivert

The personality stereotypes we often attribute to the classic salesperson are associated with the extremely extroverted individual. On the other side, we generally think of introverted people as not being fit for the rigors of the sales profession.

A 2013 study published in the journal *Psychological Science* suggests that not only are these stereotypes wrong, but there's a new personality type altogether that just might possess the best makeup for today's sales professional.

The study was conducted by researcher Adam Grant of the Wharton School at the University of Pennsylvania. Grant is the author of *Give and Take: A Revolutionary Approach to Success.*

Grant's work suggested that the best sellers are neither extroverts nor introverts. Rather, ambiverts—people who are more or less equal parts extroverted and introverted—performed best in sales in his study.

So, does this automatically count extroverts and introverts out of the sales pool? Of course not, but it does suggest both might benefit from learning how to move more toward the center. The introvert may need to consciously learn how to listen more effectively while the extrovert may need to work on more proactively challenging a prospect's assumptions.

According to Grant's research, ambiverts achieve greater sales productivity than extroverts or introverts do. Because they naturally engage in a flexible pattern of talking and listening, ambiverts are likely to express sufficient assertiveness and enthusiasm to persuade and to close a sale but are more inclined to listen to customers' interests and be less vulnerable to appearing too excited or overconfident.

The demands, skills, beliefs, and mind-set of the successful salesperson have changed so thoroughly that organizations have to rethink who they hire for this new role.

The Internet Has Reframed the Skill Set

While the onslaught of social media, content publishing, and real-time search has changed how sales and marketing roles are specifically defined, sales still owns the relationship. While it is extremely easy for the marketing department to put more and more content out there, true connection and community—the real building blocks of business relationships—are still best supplied by a person.

Throughout this book I've suggested that the fundamental purpose of a professional salesperson has evolved from closing a sale to guiding a prospect through the sales process. In that view, the function and skill set of an effective salesperson in today's content-driven environment has changed dramatically. The skills once required and, sadly, still taught in most sales training programs, are no longer applicable. The sales managers who seek to hire and train superstars are exploring, evolving, and adopting the inbound selling mind-set.

Below are some of the ways that the Internet and the changing role of the customer have changed selling, and what you need to know, as a sales coach, about the new requirements.

Listening over talking: Salespeople have always been taught to probe, listen, and offer solutions to their prospects' problems. Now they must listen intently before they ever pick up the phone, send an e-mail, or draw up a solution.

Salespeople have to monitor the social graph of a prospect in order to begin to mine for opportunities, frustrations, and buying signals. They must also be adept at constructing ways to put the pieces of information together in a package that opens doors and starts relationship building.

Insight over information: Formerly, a great deal of the salesperson's role was to deliver information. Most salespeople today face the possibility that prospects may know as much or even more about the product, service, or solution being offered than the salespeople they engage.

Today's salesperson must provide context and meaning, aggregate and filter valuable content, and become a resource of insight for the information-overloaded buyer.

Proof over promise: Price is a direct reflection of the buyer's perceived value. This doesn't always mean it's a reflection of the true value, but the ROI question will never go away unless and until an organization can show proof of value rather than promised value in their marketing materials.

Today's salesperson must commit to working deeply with clients to help measure and communicate true value received at the culmination of the sales process. With that piece in place, today's salesperson can offer proof as part of the trust-building, lead-conversion process.

Publish over prospect: Marketing departments around the world are scrambling to feed the market's expectation that they can instantly find content on any subject or need imaginable. Search engines have made consistent content production mandatory.

Few salespeople, and even fewer sales managers, view writing content as a good use of time, but it's a skill that today's successful salesperson has to embrace. Not every organization will allow their salespeople to blog, but the ones who do have the opportunity to create a stream of content informed by real-life customer stories and experiences. Smart salespeople have also begun to curate content as a way to become a resource for their clients.

Harvest over hunt: This last change probably reads as more radically different from traditional selling as any of the other factors outlined above because it sounds so passive.

Salespeople have been taught to hit the street, knock on doors, and close deals. The problem is that the street is closed, the doors are made of bits, and no one answers the phone anymore.

A hiring guide for today's sales superstar:

Hiring the right individuals and then forging them into a team based on their unique abilities is perhaps the master skill of a leader or manager. I'll turn once again to the seminal *Good to Great* to quote Jim Collins, who claims that in most organizations the trouble is not the "what" questions, it's the "who" questions.

If you want to hire someone with the skills needed to add value in today's business world, you may simply need to expand your view of who has what it takes to be a superstar.

Hire odd: I don't mean odd as in eccentric, in the oft-used sense, but you might look outside your industry or even outside the sales profession altogether to find a breed of salesperson better equipped for the demands of inbound selling. The job of selling requires both new skills and new behaviors. If your search for the next sales superstar is driven by identifying the right mind-set and behavior, you might find stars by mining individuals from other professions.

Andy Sernovitz, CEO of GasPedal and SocialMedia.org, was looking to recruit a sales force that could take his unique membership program to executives of Fortune 1000 companies. First, he ran the hiring ad below.

Ad #1—Enterprise Social Media

SocialMedia.org is looking for an experienced BtoB sales executive to sell our services to Fortune 1000 brands. We have well-qualified leads, a rich pipeline, and a supportive team.

The product is established and popular with more than 250 global brands as clients and a five-year track record in this market. This is a full-time position in our Austin office. Learn more at socialmedia.org/jobs.

After collecting resumes and interviewing some applicants, he decided that his traditional approach was turning up well-worn sales junkies with what he called too much old-fashioned sales baggage—not what he was looking for. His team decided to try a new approach and ran the ad below in an attempt to attract a different kind of applicant.

Ad #2—Community Evangelist (Membership Sales)

SocialMedia.org's Community Evangelists sell memberships in our unique community for social media executives at the world's greatest brands. We understand the challenges faced by these executives, then help them understand what we do and how it will help them succeed.

We're looking for people who like selling (but aren't salesy)—who want to do it in a positive environment for a worthy cause. Experience with selling tech/social media or memberships is helpful. We believe that the long-term relationship is more important than the short-term sale, and we're all working for the good of the organization.

The second ad was far more successful in turning up the "different" kind of applicant. Turns out the word "evangelists" attracted people who understood it from its most common context—the church. While it was not his intention, his LinkedIn ads attracted former ministers—a somewhat odd profile for a typical sales job. After interviewing several early applicants, it became clear to him that former ministers would make incredible salespeople for his membership organization.

At the time of this writing, the majority of his sales staff and his sales manager come from a religious background. Sernovitz aptly defines selling in their organization as going forth and spreading the good news about their opportunity.

Were these hires odd? Yes, they didn't fit the mold of the traditional salesperson, but they came with some interesting skills. They were empathetic, good listeners, used to presenting their ideas in public, and they filled prospects with an entirely different point of view.

I had a coworker years ago who was painfully shy—very quiet and all but absent in many discussions. But then, toward the end of long, drawn-out meetings, she would say something and the entire room would change.

She would usually start off with, "I don't know, but it seems like we should just . . ." More often than not, what followed was the profound solution to what we had all been wrestling with.

On the surface, this individual seemed to lack some of the skills many people look for, yet what she possessed was an incredible knack for leadership and strategic thinking. These are skills that are hard to teach and even harder to find. These skills—what some might call soft skills—are what make an employee valuable to your organization and they are the skills you need to look for in those you hire.

My coworker certainly fit the common notion of "freak": she was socially awkward, seemingly misplaced, and yet full of the kind of insight sorely lacking in most organizations.

Other hiring managers might have overlooked her because she didn't fit the sales mold. But you need to expand your definition of who can make a good salesperson. You need leaders, people who can make the right decisions on their own, people who can communicate complex ideas in simple ways, and people who can build relationships.

Take a good, hard look at the language you're using in your recruiting ads. Is it designed to attract the same old salespeople or is it set to attract people who think about their business from a fresh perspective?

Nonverbal skills—Much of the job of selling and relationship building is based on building trust. One of the surest ways to erode trust is incongruity—when your words and deeds don't seem to match. In selling situations people can sense incongruity; though they may not be able to articulate it, they know something doesn't add up.

Does the salesperson look you in the eye, stand confidently, shake hands firmly, and use his hands in an open and inviting manner as he speaks? This isn't the same as being outgoing; this is a much more natural, almost imperceptible skill set that fosters trust and greater communication.

There's an Emerson quote that pretty much sums this one up—"Who you are speaks so loudly I can't hear what you are saying."

Salespeople who come with customer service backgrounds and a demonstrated desire to create better customer experiences often excel in nonverbal communication. The test for good nonverbal skills starts from the moment your candidate walks in the door and greets you.

Tech inclined—You cannot make it in the world of sales (or any business, really) today without an inclination for the technical aspects of getting the job done.

Technology is used in many organizations to add efficiency to the work flow. Beyond that, it's crept into every aspect of business and our customers view its effective implementation as part of the service offering.

A technologically inclined person usually comes with social-media-strategy experience, looks for ways to use technology to create a better customer experience, and understands how to engage customers with content while still maintaining the human touch.

How technically "infused" has your interaction with a prospective hire been? Can she demonstrate social media use? Is there a way to have her provide a technical solution to a simple challenge?

Analytical—Now, this is a tricky word because it can also be a negative. You aren't necessarily looking for people who want to pore over statistics, but you do want to find people who are good at assessing needs, identifying the right decision makers, and associating economic drivers with client objectives. Salespeople should be analytical to the degree that they can effectively match the story of the client with the story of the solution. (Adding in a little "mad data scientist" never hurt anyone either.)

This might be a great place to ask a candidate to describe how he or she would go about researching a prospective customer's business.

Social proximity—If you are going to ask salespeople to sell into the C-suite of Fortune 1000 companies (and ask that they use the advice in this book to do so), spend some time finding out what connections they already have in their networks. The easiest way to do this is to view their LinkedIn profile and look for first- and second-level connections with the types of customers you need them to connect with. This may or may not be an acid test for hiring, but it's a piece of data that's becoming increasingly important.

Some sales organizations are actually making sales territory and account decisions based on this type of data as opposed to relying on traditional geographical boundaries.

Fearlessness—The sales profession has never been for the faint of heart. It's no longer for the hard-charging cold-call cowboy either. A different, more subtle kind of confidence is needed today. If your sales professionals are to be viewed by clients as guides, they need something deeper than bravado.

Salespeople need to be comfortable knocking down a few doors, for sure, but perhaps more important is the need to be comfortable challenging a prospect's assumptions, discussing value and money, and applying pressure at just the right time to elicit a yes or a no.

Fearlessness goes two ways: you need them to be fearless in the face of adversity, but also not afraid to walk away from the wrong kind of deal.

Ask prospective hires to talk about a time when they handled a price increase situation with a client. Then, ask them to talk about a time when they walked away from a prospect who demanded discounts.

Much More Than an Interview

Have you ever been wrong about a sales hire? Of course you have. Everyone has! In fact, the majority of people who attempt to make a living at selling fail. Is that because they don't know how to sell or is it because they didn't possess the passion for selling that company's products and services? I think it's the latter. I believe that anyone who believes in a product or service can effectively sell it. The challenge, then, is in hiring the right people.

Most organizations have an interview process designed to turn up good candidates, when in fact the process usually just identifies people who seem like they can sell.

If you've followed my advice in reframing the behaviors you're looking for and the types of questions you might pose to help you filter your candidates, I've got one more step for you.

Once you're convinced a candidate is a good fit, call him up and tell him that your entire team is excited about the possibility of his joining the team, but that you have one more thing for him to do. Then assign him a challenging sales scenario and ask him to prepare a sales presentation to deliver to your team and the organization's executive team in a few days. Base your challenge on your company; that is, have the prospective hire address a real need your company has. You can map out as many details as you like. By making the candidate take this test, you'll learn a great deal more about what he can actually do than what your gut told you in those interviews.

Here are a few things you're looking to learn from your challenge:

How much passion he has—It's pretty easy to fake enthusiasm for a position you're trying to land. In reality, it may not even be faking. Your candidate may believe he has a real passion for the job he is applying for. As with lots of things, though, passion may subside when it comes to actually doing the work.

How bad he wants it—If a candidate comes to your test presentation and it's pretty clear he hasn't really prepared anything of substance, he may be signaling to you that he doesn't really want this opportunity that much.

How resourceful he is—Even under the best circumstances this is a pretty big challenge, right? The potential hire might not really know that much about your company, industry, or challenges, but this is a great way to see how well he can dig, ask, research, and otherwise prepare as well as adapt on the fly.

How he performs under pressure—You haven't given him that much time to complete this challenge, and you both know that his hiring may depend on how well he completes the challenge. You need to see how well he performs under this kind of pressure—it definitely comes up in the job, after all.

How he presents—Making a pitch to an organization's executive team is an important part of the job description for a potential hire. You may not be looking for a highly tuned presentation, but a basic level of comfort (or lack of it) in this area will be revelatory. If he can't pull off this presentation in front of your team, would you feel confident sending him out to a prospect or client?

How he listens—As we discussed earlier, listening is an essential part of the job. This challenge will test how well he heard the assignment and how well he listens, engages, and crosses in his pitch.

How he reacts—You should also prepare a few common scenarios to lob at him during the test. Push him hard on price, interrupt him, and make him answer "why you?" throughout his presentation. Watch how he reacts to these questions and challenges, particularly when it comes to the topic of money.

Some might think this is a lot to ask, but you're actually doing the candidate a favor either way. You'll either put him to the test in a way that gives you some assurance that he's up to the challenge, or you'll help him figure out on his own that your organization isn't a good fit for him.

You must look for, test for, and screen for these behaviors in the quest to find your best salespeople, service people, and project people, no matter if you are hiring executive-level sales professionals or entry-level people just breaking into the business.

CHAPTER 18

Manage Automation

Sales funnel automation and lead scoring can be downright abusive these days. Companies use it, at least theoretically, to get more sales with less effort, and faster. The fact is, most companies actually use it to close off any chance that a salesperson might do better if left to develop leads that fit a less presorted and scored purchase path.

By the time a lead has made it through most people's automation funnel, she is simply shopping for the best price. Automation must be employed to let salespersons be more productive now that they are being asked to do more teaching, listening, speaking, and writing.

Automation Makes It
so You Never Have to Talk to Anyone

Technology has indeed brought us to the point where we can run a business, sell a product, and serve a customer without the need for human interaction.

This is a glorious thing, right? By throwing off the physical bonds of storefronts, full-time on premise employees, and office hours many people have been able to carve out a nontraditional living that wouldn't have been possible just a few short years ago.

But even though you can set up a business in such a way that you never have to talk to anyone, the reality is that the more we engage in automated contact, the more we crave human contact.

As our daily business transactions become cold and machine driven, we seek out and are far more receptive to the kinds of real-life interactions our conveniences separate us from. This has created an opportunity that smart salespeople and marketers can seize.

Think about a typical marketing- or sales-related engagement these days. You get an e-mail urging you to sign up for an online seminar. You fill out the form, get an e-mail confirmation, miss the call because you know you'll get the recording, download the recording and put it in a digital folder . . . where it sits today, unplayed.

Heck, I do this all the time, so there's no judgment here; I'm simply recognizing the reality.

Where's the opportunity in this kind of automation? What if you started adding human engagement back into some of the automated routines? What if you started shocking people by asking them what they wanted, not telling them what you were offering? What if you took the time and energy to warmly greet and welcome people into your communities?

Let's go back to the idea of the online seminar above.

Imagine that someone enrolls in your online seminar. You could pick up the phone and thank them personally for signing up, confirm the time-zone conversion for them, and offer them some material that would make the call even more useful.

Something tells me that the prospect who gets that call is going to be more likely to attend and to pay just a little more attention to what's being said and offered.

Now, let's say a prospect signs up for that session, but doesn't end up attending the live online event. What if, when he got back to the office the next morning, he received a call letting him know where to get the recording and how to get the transcript as well. Again, I'm thinking that prospect is going to respond positively, if only because no one extends that kind of personal follow-up anymore.

Not everyone wants a phone call, but a growing number of people will be open to personal contact, especially because it adds value. They may be so taken by the effort that they'll feel obligated to see what else you've got in store for them. And that's the point—this being human stuff means you're going to need to raise the bar on everything.

My friend Jonathan Fields, founder of the Good Life Project, shared this automated e-mail he received from a company after making a purchase.

> Hey,
>
> Thank you so much for your purchase, it's a pleasure doing business with you.
>
> We would greatly appreciate some positive feedback.
>
> All the best,

Kind of makes you feel all warm and fuzzy, right? Well, here's what Jonathan had to say about the impression he got:

> Amazing that companies send out stuff like this. Here's what my brain actually read:
>
> Hey, faceless sack of cash. Thank you for giving us your money, we really enjoyed taking it. Now, go tell everyone how delicious we are at giving you what you asked for. And if we weren't great, please pretend it never happened, we don't want to hear it and don't even think of telling anyone. Huggies & bunny rabbits, Faceless Retailer

Turn the tide of technology-saturated marketing to your favor by being the company that actually delivers value and shows appreciation for every single member of your community.

You can build and add human touchpoints as internal systems initially, then as you perfect them and grow, use those external resources to scale.

This is how you stand out and stay close enough to your list of customers (people) to discover what they need and want. The human touch turns your best customers into raving fans.

Social Collaboration Tools

After spending the first part of this chapter bemoaning the fact that overdependence on automated technology can remove the human element, I want to switch gears and talk about tools that can actually help you be more human.

Test some of the tools I recommend below. If you like them, and they work for your business, share them with your salespeople. You can use them to strengthen the efficiency and level of cooperation of your own team and to connect with clients and prospects on a more human level.

It's not the tool that removes genuine interaction; it's the way people choose to use the tool that's the problem. When you employ a tool in a way that actually adds value or creates convenience—for example, a scheduling app—you can actually make the experience more human.

One thing is for certain—it's become much easier to work virtually these days. New online apps and tools are being created every day to make it easier to connect, collaborate, and contribute and to manage staff now flung far and wide of the traditional cube or office setting.

Tools that allow users to meet instantly using video, discuss and edit documents in real time, clip and store notes and ideas for team sharing, and create custom content on the fly for individual clients and industry segments have enabled even the smallest businesses to do things relatively inexpensively that only a few years ago would have cost tens of thousands of dollars.

I enjoy finding and using these new tools. Over the last year or so, I've noticed a trend in these tools—they've become more social. In other words, they seem to be taking clues from social networks and the pattern of sharing, "liking," and commenting the networks have fostered to create social collaboration as a central theme.

Below are some relatively new entries to the collaboration and accountability tool set that share some of these new, more social, attributes.

Evernote Business—Evernote Business gives employees all the Evernote tools to save and find everything that matters in their day-to-day lives, while also providing the centralized management features businesses need.

iDoneThis—Sometimes working with remote teams makes it hard to keep up on projects or even to consider how much work people are putting in because you don't witness it in action. iDoneThis is a very simple e-mail-based team productivity management tool that prompts everyone on a project or team to reply to an e-mail reminder with what they did that day. The next day, the iDoneThis administrator gets a digest with what everyone on the team got done.

KanbanFlow—the problem with most project management software is that it's just too complicated to figure out quickly. KanbanFlow is as lean and intuitive as they come. It presents project boards and to-do lists in a very visual way and leans heavily on the Pomodoro time management school of thought that suggests you work in twenty-five-minute bursts with five-minute mental breaks between.

WalkMe—This tool is really more about collaborating with customers, but I love what it does. WalkMe allows you to create step-by-step guides that show your customer (or any website visitor) how to do what you want her to do. It inserts little instruction bubbles that guide your user to the next task.

A Web Whiteboard—As the name implies, this is a whiteboard on the web. It takes advantage of some nice HTML5 functionality and is a dead simple way to collaborate on drawing. I can imagine some nice whiteboarding on big screens as a cheap alternative to computer-driven Smart Boards.

Co-meeting—This tool bills itself as a new-style group communication tool. Basically it allows you to hold text-based group discussions in which everyone participates via chat. What I like about this tool is the way it creates and saves multiple threads and shows a comment being created in real time, much like a real conversation. This format won't be for everyone, but it offers benefits that you can't find in face-to-face meetings, such as logging everything that is said.

Podio—Podio is a project management, CRM, sales, and intranet multitool that clearly takes its design from social networks. You can create an instant social intranet site that's completely customizable to your organization and manage events, meetings, collaboration, and client communication all in one workspace.

In addition there are thousands of add-on apps being built for the platform.

Peak—Peak is the automated way to keep track of what everyone is working on. Peak takes a slightly different approach: you don't download or visit an app, you simply connect the productivity apps that everyone already uses and then you can monitor how much time was spent on things like e-mail and social media.

Scoop.it—Most people wouldn't call this a collaboration tool, but I think it has great potential as one. Scoop.it allows you to curate content from around the Web and build a custom magazine with it. You can bring in all your social networks and share with all your social networks.

What makes this a potential collaboration tool is that you can discover ways to cocurate with your customers and community members.

Imagine having your customers from a specific industry contributing to an industry-specific magazine.

Addvocate—Addvocate is a great way for companies to manage the way their employees promote their brand online. It gives companies tools to coach employees on how to spread the right message throughout their social networks.

The way we work has changed dramatically and permanently, so let's celebrate that idea by employing tools that make our work even more useful, consistent, and enriching.

Conclusion:
The New World of Selling Awaits

started this book by posing the idea that, in the traditional model, marketing owned the message of any given business, while sales owned the relationships. Today, however, who owns what is terribly blurred.

One of my primary objectives in writing this book was to change the context of selling. I hope you've seen that the traditional context of selling must be blown to pieces, not because I want it to change, but because we have to rethink what salespeople actually need to do to be effective in today's market.

Selling has changed because the world of buying has changed. The only question that remains is whether you will use what you've learned in this book to race to catch up with this ever-moving world.

The new world of selling awaits; it should be pretty obvious that there's no time to lose learning how to operate in it. While it may make good conversation to set up the ideas in this new world with the catchphrase "marketing is the new selling," it would be foolish, at this point, to hold on to that distinction. It's greater than that. What we know now is that inbound selling is simply the new selling, and that "always be connecting" is the replacement for "always be closing."

Listening, educating, sharing, nurturing, curating, observing, and deconstructing are the new pillars of value delivery in the new world of selling. Providing insight, mining networks, building authority, and measuring impact are the foundational skills required to excel in the new world of selling.

The new sales professional is an information-gathering, insight-filtering, socially connected thought leader who just *happens* to think like a marketer and sell like a superstar!

Now that you're armed with all the tools and mind-sets required for skillfully selling in the new world, what are you waiting for? Let's go sell something.

ACKNOWLEDGMENTS

Carol for patience beyond what is deserved

My girls for keeping me always appreciative

My dad for teaching me how to sell

My mom for teaching me how to smile in the face of anything

Steve for pushing this out into the world

Natalie for incredibly smart editing

Duct Tape Marketing Consultant Network for tireless support

Anyone who sells for a living for stopping, even if just for a moment, to consider another way!

Let's Collaborate

Be sure to visit the companion website for this book at ducttapesell ing.com. I would love to hear your stories, challenges, and observations regarding the strategies, tactics, and tools contained in *Duct Tape Selling*.

Reach out and share examples of your blogging, networking, and authority-building evidence. And by all means, share your sales adventures and misadventures as you rage out into the new world of selling.

I consider you a member of the Duct Tape Selling community now and I encourage you to connect with me online.

- Duct Tape Selling online—ducttapeselling.com
- John Jantsch on Twitter—twitter.com/ducttape
- John Jantsch on Facebook—facebook.com/ducttapemarketing
- John Jantsch on LinkedIn—linkedin.com/in/ducttapemarketing
- John Jantsch on Google+—plus.google.com/+JohnJantsch

INDEX